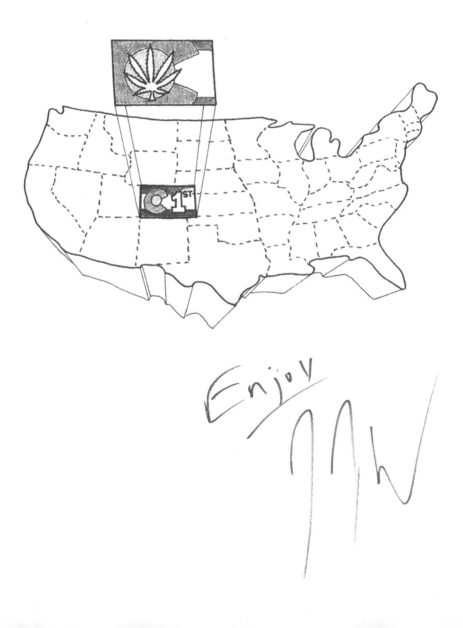

Enjoy

WEEDGALIZED IN COLORADO

TRUE TALES FROM THE HIGH COUNTRY

JOHNNY WELSH

Peak 1 Publishing, LLC
Frisco, Colorado

For Mom, who stressed the
importance of a good education,
and for Dad, who paid for it.

"Yesterday, Colorado Governor John Hickenlooper signed an amendment that officially legalized marijuana in the state. Stoners took a moment to thank Governor Hickenlooper—then they spent a few hours just saying the word 'Hickenlooper.'"

—Jimmy Fallon, *Late Night with Jimmy Fallon*, December 2012

Contents

Disclaimer

This book is designed to entertain and inform about the subject matter. It is sold with the understanding that the author, contributing authors, artists, those quoted, and the publisher are not rendering any legal advice.

Laws and regulations, especially those at the local level can change at any time. If legal or other expert assistance is required, the services of legal counsel should be sought. Check with local authorities regarding the local laws and ordinances in your town or a town you may be visiting.

Every effort has been made to check the facts for accuracy. However, there may be typographical or content errors. Therefore, this book should be used primarily for entertainment purposes.

Keep in mind that the legal cannabis industry is not without its restrictions and each state has its own local laws. It is a subject with a lot of gray areas still, so it's best to refrain from consumption until you have checked with law enforcement or legal counsel.

Author's Note

I'm a bartender. For nearly two decades, I've earned my living mixing and serving drinks in Frisco, Colorado, in the heart of Colorado ski country.

Frisco, a tiny mountain town, is an undiscovered gem compared to its more worldly neighbors like Aspen, Vail, and Breckenridge. Our little town sits in the middle of seven of some of the best ski mountains in the state, and our summers are quite beautiful.

I work in several local bars. People tend to talk pretty openly to bartenders. I have seen and heard the finest people doing the poorest things, and the poorest in character doing the finest things. I make no comments on what I see, and keep private things private. People ask me about sports, sex, psychology, local activities, where to park, where to eat, stocks, and wait, oh yes, sex again.

Even so, I was unprepared for the volume of questions and stories that arose about the cannabis industry when Coloradans voted, on November 6, 2012, to legalize pot. Customer curiosity exploded when the bill became law, and the first recreational pot shops opened January 1, 2014. I was *overwhelmed* by the amount of discussion. Never before had there been this much fervor behind a topic discussed at the bars where I work. Interest has yet to wane.

For years, my favorite greeting to visitors, tourists, and new arrivals was, "Welcome to the high country." I was referring to the elevation and especially the grandeur of our beautiful state. We have the highest elevated city in the country

(Leadville, 10,430 feet); the highest paved road (on Mt. Evans, 14,258 feet); and the highest highway tunnel (Eisenhower Tunnel, 11,000 feet). But now "the high country" has a whole new meaning.

Stories . . . I Get Stories

It didn't take me long to realize I was in a unique position to provide an eyewitness report on the real-world impact of Colorado's marijuana laws. The stories I heard from my customers, a broad mix of locals and tourists, covered an unusual breadth and depth of experiences. They ranged from the uneasy feelings about legalization to the nonstop search for new ways to find both fun and profit in legal weed. I was dying to share these stories and to hear more. It was time to get out from behind the bar.

Out from Behind the Bar

I began to compile my favorite anecdotes from the bar, and I pulled together a team of great people to help me brainstorm topics and collect interviews. We knew there were obvious people to talk with, like dispensary owners, but we also wanted to learn more about the people impacted by legalization who weren't in the public eye. People like the proprietors of new, related businesses, and the budtenders, the nurses, the illegal dealers, and even the "Town Stoner."

Some of the team are in the food and beverage industry, one is in the computer industry, and a few are entrepreneurs. One of us has never smoked marijuana, one has in the past but doesn't anymore, two are casual or rare users, and one is a regular user. We set up a mastermind meeting and created a mission: to deliver lighthearted, grassroots (yes, yes, I know) accounts of an unprecedented event—the legalization of marijuana in Colorado and its first eighteen months of mayhem.

What to Expect

If you're looking for a definitive guidebook or journalistic investigation, this isn't the book for you. As I said, I'm a bartender. But on the other hand, if you want to learn what it's really like to live in the first state in America to legalize marijuana, you're probably in the right place. You'll find answers to the questions my customers ask all the time: "Hey, how is it *really* going over there?" "Is it reefer madness?" "Are there people coming in from all over because of it?" "Has crime gone up or down?" "Do they really make gummy bears with pot in them?" "What is it like going into a pot shop?"

I won't tell you how to open a dispensary or make a living in this fledgling industry, but you'll glean plenty of tips from glimpses into the minds of people who are already doing just that. You'll find stories from people who make their living solely from this newly legalized industry: the business tycoon, the cannabis strain expert, the franchise guru, the medical healer, the promoter, and the cannabis activist.

You'll also find stories like the guy who bought the entire town of Stoner, CO, and plans to pump in almost $100 million to redevelop and create a research facility. I talked with three film crews: one is a reality show, a comedy, and the other is a documentary on cannabis topics in Colorado. I interviewed a sheriff.

Many talented writers are reporting on this hot topic, and I reprint some of their stories. I do provide some practical information, too. In the appendices, you'll see some of the new laws and guidelines, names of different strains of cannabis, pot stocks, favorite dispensaries, and many of the nicknames of marijuana.

Believe me, I am no expert on cannabis. When I was growing up, there was only "seed weed" and "good bud." Now, there are more strains of weed than lawyers in New Jersey, with creative names like Sour Diesel, Skunk, Northern Lights, Bubba Kush, Blueberry Haze, Ferrari, California Dream, and wax concentrates named Bruce Banner and Harlequin, and thousands more. There are websites dedicated to the different types of strains, names, and what kind of high they will give you, in addition to the definitions and differences of *indicas* and *sativas*.

By the way, the word *cannabis* seems to now be the most commonly used term for marijuana. Both are used throughout this book interchangeably.

Why Does a Bartender Write a Book?

I anticipate many questions from those who are against the legalization of pot. The opposition still runs surprisingly deep. I slammed into it headfirst when I tried to donate a percent of sales from this book to charity. I tried five different charities and was turned down by each one. Five out of five would not accept money from the "marijuana industry."

Mostly, I wrote this book to entertain and inform—to give you a catbird seat at the bar during the first year of legalization.

These stories were the most talked about while I was mixing and serving drinks. There are more stories out there. They are never ending. If I have another agenda, it may be this: in my twenty-two years as a bartender, I've witnessed the effects of alcohol on people every day. Now that cannabis is legal, I'm now face-to-face not just with people who are drunk, but also with people who are high. I see the similarities and the differences. I know firsthand what each drug can do to people. By raising awareness of the effects of both drink and marijuana on users, positive and negative, I hope to alleviate some fears. I hope to ease flamboyant use of the weed by those who push the boundaries of the new law, but I also hope my bias comes through. In my simple bartender's eye view, drinkers tend to get emotional, and smokers tend to get happy. (And hungry)

CHAPTER 1

The Great Colorado Pot Scramble

Hemp is of first necessity to the wealth
and protection of the country.
—Thomas Jefferson, U.S. President quote on hemp

Be It Enacted by the People of the State of Colorado...

Colorado Amendment 64, known as the "Regulate Marijuana like Alcohol" act, showed up on our ballots in 2012.

Voters were asked to vote "Yes" or "No" to the following question:

> Shall there be an amendment to the Colorado con-
> stitution concerning marijuana, and, in connection
> therewith, providing for the regulation of marijuana;
> permitting a person twenty-one years of age or older
> to consume or possess limited amounts of marijuana;
> providing for the licensing of cultivation facilities,
> product manufacturing facilities, testing facilities, and
> retail stores; permitting local governments to regulate

or prohibit such facilities; requiring the general assembly to enact an excise tax to be levied upon wholesale sales of marijuana; requiring that the first $40 million in revenue raised annually by such tax be credited to the public school capital construction assistance fund; and requiring the general assembly to enact legislation governing the cultivation, processing, and sale of industrial hemp?[1]

On November 6, 2012, we voted yes. We had little idea what we were unleashing.

Cannabis is now regulated similarly to the way alcohol is regulated, with the twenty-one and over laws. People are also allowed to grow up to six plants, three immature and three mature plants per legal age person per household. That might be a higher ratio of immature to mature than some of us adults. (I know I fall in the immature category—my girlfriend reminds of this often!)

Colorado adults over twenty-one can possess up to one ounce of marijuana as well. Driving under the influence of marijuana is illegal. Employers in the state of Colorado can also restrict the use of marijuana on the job by its employees by way of their company policy.

And the "Green Rush," Colorado's great social experiment, has come rolling in, with hordes of people from around the world scrambling to cash in on Colorado's newest cash crop.

Selling cannabis is still considered to be a very risky business, as it is illegal on the federal level, but that hasn't stemmed the tide of entrepreneurs. With almost all of the state licenses already taken from the limited supply, the magnitude of the efforts to cash in on this industry astonished me. New businesses that popped up include dispensaries, growing operations, T-shirts, stickers, paraphernalia, advice on legal aspects, consulting, stocks, vaporizers, air filtration, packaging, horticulture classes, pot tourism, dispensary classes, festivals, tours, clipping and trimming, budtending, and that is just the tip of a very large iceberg.

Pot tourism is also very real. Couples young and old tell me they're "pot tourists" when they come into my bar to have a snack at happy hour. Will it rival the ski industry? The cannabis industry sold over $700 million in the first year with approximately $44 million collected in taxes. Projections are predicted at $1 billion in sales for 2016. Ski tourism is currently around $2.5 billion.

"Could recreational marijuana business surpass ski industry?"

VAIL — You have to admire the optimism of Colorado's ganjapreneurs who say the state's legal pot industry could generate more money than skiing in a few years. "Skiing pumps about $3 billion annually in Colorado's economy," says Jennifer Rudolph, communications director with Colorado Ski Country USA. "Hunting, fishing and watchable wildlife tourism adds another $3 billion," says the state's Division of Parks and Wildlife.

"By 2018, Colorado's legal reefer could eclipse both," they say, "and they're taking a nationwide view." Cannabis venture capitalists Arcview Investor Network is projecting nationwide legal pot revenues of $10 billion by 2018.[2]

Colorado and Washington State are two experiments right now, and the whole world is watching and waiting. Alaska, Oregon, and Washington, DC, have also passed legalized recreational use while this book was being written. Other states are looking to see how much money is being made and if problems arise. After all, the prohibition of marijuana dates back almost seventy-five years.

In times like these all we can do is watch and see if "Reefer Madness" ensues or if other states follow suit. These are unprecedented times.

CHAPTER 2

A Brief History of Pot

What do you call a pothead who doesn't inhale?
Mr. President.

Since ancient times weed has been around and used as a source to reach euphoria. Its medical history runs side by side with recreational use. Chinese folk medicine, with records as far back as 2737 BC, used the herb for a number of ailments. Demand for its use spread around the world quickly—first from China to India, then to North Africa. Colonial North America didn't want to be left out, so hemp was introduced as a huge source of fiber.

References to the hemp plant appear as early as 2600 BC in ancient Chinese manuscripts. In 1545, European explorers arrived in the New World to find the plant growing wild. Along with corn, wheat, and other crops, marijuana was considered to be so useful that early Jamestown settlers in 1607 began its cultivation.

In the early 1600s, it was introduced in England. Eventually, it gained worldwide use as a household drug for treating menstrual cramps, common headaches, and a host of other ailments.

Hemp is one of the oldest psychoactive plants to color our early planet. Fans of pot have been inhaling the dried leaves of the plant and ingesting them for pleasure and medical use for centuries.

A Few Interesting Historical Facts[3]

- Marijuana use as medicine was first recorded as far back as 2727 BC by the Chinese Emperor Shen Nung. He documented its medical effectiveness in treating rheumatism, gout, and even absentmindedness.

- Queen Victoria of England was prescribed cannabis for menstrual cramps by her personal physician, Sir Russell Reynolds. He wrote in the first issue of *The Lancet*, in 1890, "when pure and administered carefully, cannabis is one of the most useful medicines we possess."

- America's first marijuana law was not, as many might imagine, to ban the growing of the plant. Back in 1619, farmers in the Jamestown Colony in Virginia were "ordered" to grow hemp crops. This was the first of many such laws. Also, between 1763 and 1767, not growing the hemp plant could get a farmer fined or thrown in jail.

- The reason for encouraging hemp farming was so very different from the reasons that many people try to grow it today. Back then the hemp plant had more practical uses. Once harvested, it was turned into clothing, sails, and rope.

- Hemp was once considered legal tender in the United States, even accepted by the government as a payment for taxes.

- President George Washington cultivated Indian hemp (cannabis *sativa indica*, which was medical cannabis that could also be used for fiber, although not as well as regular hemp) on his farm. In a letter to his farm manager, he wrote, "Make the most you can of the Indian hemp seed. Sow it everywhere." Visitors to the 1876 American Centennial Exposition in Philadelphia were invited to "toke up" at the Turkish Hashish Exposition stand.

- In the 1890s, several women's temperance societies actually recommended the use of hashish instead of alcohol. Their reasoning: liquor led to domestic violence, whereas hashish did not.

- Prior to 1910, the growth and trade of marijuana (and hashish—a resinous substance produced by the flowering parts of the plant) was fairly limited. However, following the conclusion of the Mexican Revolution, trafficking of the drug opened up, making growth and transport of the drug easier and more profitable. The business expanded to reach the ports of New Orleans where it was sold on the black market, alongside other strains of the plant. It wasn't long before the trend of marijuana use began to overshadow the historic applications of cannabis as a medicine.

- The drug became popular in the '50s, '60s, and '70s (especially its stronger derivatives, such as hashish, charas, ghanja, and bhang) among musicians who maintained that smoking marijuana gave them the inspiration they needed to play their music. These musicians glamorized the use of marijuana. Some claimed it gave them contemplative vision and a feeling of overwhelming freedom and verve. Others not only used the drug but also sold it to a variety of customers. As entertainers went on the road, so did their drugs. Eventually, use of marijuana, alcohol, and other mind-altering drugs spread and soon became prevalent in major cities worldwide, such as Chicago, New York, London, and Paris.

- History shows that many of the musicians and entertainers of the Jazz Age, who used drugs and alcohol, relied heavily on gangland kings for their "gigs" (jobs). Frequently, these gangsters were able to provide (for a fee) a variety of drugs and bootleg alcohol for the performers and their staffs.

- Up until the 1940s, marijuana was easily obtained at the local general store or pharmacy. Used as a medicine, it was listed in the *United States Pharmacopoeia* as useful for medical conditions such as nausea, rheumatism, and labor pain. It was subsequently removed from the pharmacopoeia in 1942 when it was determined that marijuana was a harmful and addictive drug, causing psychotic episodes.

– In many parts of the United States marijuana is the number one cash crop. This is mostly because of the high prices it gets on the black market.

– The word *marijuana* is a Mexican slang term. It became popular in the late 1930's in America during a series of media and government programs that we now refer to as the "Reefer Madness Movement." It refers specifically to the part of cannabis that Mexican soldiers used to smoke.

– There is about half a gram of marijuana in a single joint. Marijuana is the most often used illegal drug in the United States.

COLORADO CANNABIS FAQ

Keep in mind that any rules, laws, or regulations published in this book are subject to change and any questions regarding the legalities of your town or county should be directed to your local authorities or town clerk.

Who can purchase recreational marijuana?

Anyone twenty-one and older, with a valid government ID, is allowed to purchase, smoke, and possess marijuana in Colorado. Much like in a liquor store, individuals need to show an ID in order to make purchases. You can share with a friend, as long as you aren't getting paid in the process.[4]

Where and when can people purchase marijuana?

Licensed retail shops began selling recreational marijuana on January 1, 2014. The shops were previously medical marijuana dispensaries and may or may not have chosen to continue to sell medical products in addition to retail products. Shops have hours mandated by the state, much like liquor stores, so no purchases can be made before 8:00 am.[5]

How much can individuals buy?

In a single transaction, Colorado residents twenty-one and over can purchase up to one ounce, while out-of-state visitors can purchase one-quarter ounce. Researchers have concluded the average joint contains slightly less than one-half a gram of marijuana. An ounce is slightly more than 28 grams, so one ounce equals approximately 60 joints.[6]

Can people take marijuana out of Colorado?

Definitely not. Every city and county in Colorado has its own marijuana regulations. It is illegal to leave Colorado with any marijuana products. Additionally, Denver International Airport has chosen to ban the possession, use, display, and transfer (giving to another person) of all marijuana on its property.[7]

CHAPTER 3

A New World

*When I was in England, I experimented with marijuana
a time or two, and I didn't like it and didn't inhale
and never tried it again.*
—Gov. Bill Clinton, New York, March 29,
during the 1992 Campaign

In the upcoming chapters, I'll tell you all sorts of tales about the first year of legalization, which I've compiled by interviewing many key players on the scene at the time. I thought it only fitting that I open with my own experience: a step-by-step walk-through of what buying pot in those early days was like.

For me, it first felt real on the night of the actual vote—November 6, 2012. A group of friends and I had planned on meeting up at Ollie's Pub and Grub in Frisco after we voted. Around 7:00 or 8:00 p.m. that evening, the televisions in the bar began to show some voting results. I will never forget how loudly the whole bar cheered. Marijuana had just become legal in the state of Colorado in regulated amounts for adults over twenty-one. It was a standing ovation. I don't think I have even heard of a standing ovation happening as a result of the passage of a bill. A mere fourteen months later, legalized cannabis became available to purchase in dispensaries across the state.

On January 1, 2014, the day the first recreational pot shops opened in our state, I was having an early lunch with some friends in Frisco, and we decided to go to the local pot shop to purchase marijuana simply because it was legal. I am a very rare consumer of cannabis, so it didn't matter to me either way. It was just crazy to see and attempt to be a part of day one in history. We all wanted to post a photo on Facebook holding up our little bags of weed for our friends in other states to see. Can you think of a better way to make some friends green with envy?

The pot shop was so crowded and there was such a long line that we changed our minds and left empty-handed. The next day, the front page of the paper showed pictures of the long lines at the pot shops all across the state. Reports of how these shops were running out of product were rampant.

The New World of the Dispensary

About five weeks after the opening day of cannabis sales, we finally made it in. The experience of walking into a marijuana dispensary after January 1, 2014 was as surreal as one could possibly imagine.

Here is how it all works. You walk in and are greeted by a front-desk receptionist. (In the city of Denver, you must first pass through security guards at some of the dispensaries.) The receptionists all have a smile the size of the Cheshire cat. You are asked to show your identification card proving that you

are over the age of twenty-one. After those formalities, it is
time to wait your turn to walk into the recreational side of the
dispensary. (Most dispensaries have two separate rooms: one
for medical card carriers and the other for recreational use.)
To enter the recreational side, you only need to show an
accepted form of ID. For the medical side, you must show
your ID plus your medical marijuana card, which is state
issued and prescribed by a physician.

When your turn comes up, you are escorted into a room
with display cases full of jars containing many strains of
marijuana. There can be anywhere from five to twenty jars,
depending on the supply. You are allowed to smell the
merchandise but can't touch. The budtender behind the
counter will guide you through your legal marijuana purchasing experience. They rattle off terms like *indica* and *sativa* and
all the creative names for the different strains. Introductions
are given to the hundreds of new products as well, such as
edibles, tinctures, sprays, salves, creams, saps, and topical oils.
You are asked what your goal is when you consume cannabis.
In other words, what kind of high do you want, or what do
you want from your cannabis experience? After the budtender's
descriptions, you choose the type and the amount, up to one
ounce for Colorado residents.

At the register, your product is placed in a childproof
container if it's not already in one. You pay with cash or debit
card since there are no credit cards accepted at dispensaries
at this time.

The folks in front of and behind me giggled when they
received their packages. These are unprecedented times here
in Colorado, and the dispensary experience is one that can

be enjoyed by all. Not everyone who enters is required to purchase. I went in to see this new world of marijuana sales. I didn't purchase anything on that particular day. I didn't have cash on me.

My First Taste of Colorado Cannabis

My first purchase was sometime in late February 2014. I was not ready for how strong cannabis had become since my college days, long ago.

I tried it that night before meeting up with my coworkers at the 5th Avenue Grille in Frisco. They were working, and I was supposed to meet them as they were finishing up. As I was walking, it began to snow and the weed began to kick in. I was just a block away from the restaurant when I stopped walking. Was I too stoned to socialize? Should I go home? I stood at the one block mark, in the snow, and agonized about what to do. After reaching my "big life" decision to go home and watch a movie, I turned around and went back up the hill toward home.

What I didn't know was that all my coworkers were standing in the front window watching the snow fall. They also watched me walk up, stand on the corner for five minutes, then turn around, and walk back home. My cell phone rang.

"What the hell are you doing out there in the snow?" they asked when I picked up. I started to laugh. I knew I was busted. I managed to tell them what I did, and I could hear uproarious laughter through the phone.

CHAPTER 4

Meet the Ganjapreneurs

What do you call money that grows on trees?
Marijuana

Colorado has had its share of rushes. First there was the silver rush and gold rush, and now we are in the midst of the green rush. With this new rush there has been a large influx of new residents, changes in laws, and a mad dash to be part of the money story. Almost every day there is an article in the newspaper or segment on the news dealing with the amount of money being made from the legalization of marijuana. There is a scramble by entrepreneurs, nicknamed *ganjapreneurs*, to cash in on this new rush. In the gold rush days, it wasn't just those who were striking gold that were cashing in. There were those that made exceptional livings selling picks and shovels. What will be the picks and shovels of this latest rush? Stay tuned for stories of some of the ancillary businesses popping up in hordes right now.

The following story wasn't a Colorado story, but this one must be told.

Girl Scout Story

"I don't always buy Girl Scout cookies, but when I do, I buy them from the genius outside The Green Cross pot dispensary."[8]

According to the story I quoted from above, written by Jenn Harris in the *LA Times* on February 21, 2014, a Girl Scout in San Francisco, California, set up her Girl Scout cookie table outside a medical marijuana dispensary and sold about 117 boxes of cookies in less than two hours. The controversy that ensued ranged from support of the sales genius to complaints that her location was inappropriate for the Girl Scouts of America. The Colorado chapter of the Girl Scouts issued a statement: "Our Girl Scouts are not allowed to sell cookies in front of marijuana shops or liquor stores/bars." Wow! Did this story cause a stir or what? The Girl Scout's success was a testament to what realtors always say: "It's all about location, location, location."

And if you think that story is genius, a recreational/medical dispensary just opened up in December in between a barbecue restaurant and Taco Bell in Frisco, Colorado! (See Native Roots Dispensary interview with Rhett Jordan on page 90.) Incidentally, the Native Roots Dispensary replaced a fast-food restaurant that was known for displaying bible scripture on the front marquis on the highway. Many locals find this very amusing.

The Colorado Ganjapreneurs

- Philip Wolf
- Ryan Collins
- Ste-V Day
- Betty and Bonnie
- Jessica Catalano
- Bud + Breakfast team

Cultivating Spirits

Contact Information:

Philip Wolf

CEO/Founder

www.CultivatingSpirits.com

info@CultivatingSpirits.com.

970-368-2446

Meet our first ganjapreneur, Philip Wolf, CEO/Founder of Cultivating Spirits, a multifaceted cannabis tour company that aims to (per its website) "set itself apart by providing responsible, educational, and spirited cannabis experiences."

The company donates five percent of its profits through its "Spirit Forward" program.

On May 3, 2014, I attended a dinner provided by Cultivating Spirits. The company offers education about the cannabis industry, coupled with lessons in "responsible consumption," a gourmet three-course dinner paired with both wine and cannabis, and a dispensary tour. All this comes with limousine rides though one of the most scenic drives in Summit County.

I was blown away once again by the creative endeavors that people are coming up with in this new industry. Philip Wolf, his partner Nick Brown, and their team were quite impressive. During my visit, they left no detail unattended. From the initial introductions to the volume of the background music, they had it dialed in.

Here's a quick rundown of my evening event. We met the tour leader and our fellow adventurers at the Cultivating Spirits Eatery, where we were also given the evening's itinerary.

The first hour was the food demo. The evening began with a cooking demonstration complete with instructions. The food prepared did not contain cannabis, but instead was "paired" with it. Do you know what a cannabis pairing is? I sure didn't.

As Philip Wolf told us, "A cannabis pairing is where they pair the terpene profiles of cannabis with the flavor profiles of food for a harmonizing effect. Terpenes are what gives cannabis its distinct smell and also provides mood benefits. Think of essential oils."

Places were set up around the chef's prep area, with linen napkins set out and ice water already poured. We were offered a glass of wine to enjoy during the first course.

We watched the chef create a sesame seared ahi tuna and avocado tower over buckwheat noodles, and an Alaskan crab spring citrus salad with fresh melon and soy reduction. He described each step and, after explaining how he planned to prepare the main course and dessert and confirming that no one had any food allergies, served us the mini sculpture and salad as our appetizers.

We were an eclectic group of ten, and we all got to know each other a bit as we ate our appetizers. I don't know why, but no matter where I go, every time I say I'm from New Jersey, everybody laughs.

Next came the limousine ride over to the dispensary, where we were educated on the many new marijuana products that are available and how to consume them responsibly. Definitions of new terms were provided, and our guide led a question and answer session. The cannabis technicians described the strain of cannabis that they had paired up with the dinner entrée our chef had planned. We didn't consume any cannabis in the dispensary. There were multiple viewing windows where we could see the cannabis being grown. Growth has to be done in a very sterile and controlled environment, so we could only look through a window. Tours in the grow room were not allowed due to contamination issues.

Another scenic limousine ride took us to a wine tasting, where we tasted the four wines that could be paired with the evening's entrée. After a question and answer session, we were taken on yet another scenic ride in our limousine to where a "cannabis tasting" was held. I learned to look for the differences in taste on the inhalation and exhalation. I was also taught cupping (the act of moving saliva around in the mouth), which coffee roasters do to get the overall flavor.

Our last stop was back at the Cultivating Spirits Eatery for the gourmet entrée and dessert that was inspired by the cannabis du jour, which was called Grape Ape. The food was amazing, and so was the pot later in the evening. Cultivating Spirits Eatery uses local and organic produce and meats whenever in season or feasible. Our entrée was Black Angus tournedos of filet mignon with smoked salmon, mashed potatoes, and caramelized Brussels sprouts with Zinfandel Beurre Rouge. (I will be making this one at home from the notes I took.) For dessert, we had molten chocolate lava cake with sweet butter lace cookies, double vanilla ice cream, and fresh strawberries.

Cultivating Spirits tours can be booked with groups of up to ten people on their site.

The quote of the night came from staff member Angelique Justich as we were eating fresh strawberries, "You have to beat the deer and the hippies if you want to get some wild strawberries. They only last a week."

Aspen Canyon Ranch

Contact Information:
Ryan Collins
13206 County Road 3
Parshall, CO 80468
www.AspenCanyon.com
info@AspenCanyon.com
970-725-3600

I took a forty-minute drive north to meet with Ryan Collins, owner of Aspen Canyon Ranch. In one of the most scenic drives in our area, the road to the ranch climbs over Ute Pass (pronounced yoot) and past historic Henderson Mining Company and Mill. (To this day, I can't drive over Ute pass without hearing in my head Joe Pesci from *My Cousin Vinny* saying, ". . . these two yoots.") There are little pullouts on the side of the road all the way up to the summit where cars have pulled off to photograph some of the breathtaking views. No matter how many times I drive over there, I find myself stopping as well to take in all the beauty and grandeur.

The last half of the road leading to the ranch is unpaved. Arriving at the ranch, the first sights to be seen, other than the cool ranch entrance signs, are the horses and the corrals. Next is the family of goats, followed by the piggies. This place is a paradise off the beaten path in the remote area of Parshall, twenty-six miles north of Silverthorne, Colorado. Lodging for guests consists of riverside cabins, a river house, a cliff house, and camping. So far, Ryan is planning a few music festivals here for the summers and expanding in the future. There is plenty of land and space for camping, and lodging is available. Adults can enjoy the music while still following laws, such as not driving after consumption.

Owner Ryan Collins came up with the idea for adding vacation packages designed for cannabis users around January 1, 2014, when recreational marijuana was first legalized. Now, during designated days, special arrangements can be made for those over twenty-one who wish to include cannabis during their all-inclusive stay. Activities include horseback riding, ATV rentals, skeet shooting, fishing, hiking, and relaxing, as well as being allowed to smoke marijuana freely on the grounds as long as special arrangements have been made in advance. There aren't many places in the world right now that can offer such a vacation as remote as this ranch, with the Williams Fork River running through it.

When asked about any changes in business that has happened since January 1, 2014, Ryan said that he's getting a lot of phone calls from large groups in Florida, Texas, New York, North Carolina, South Carolina, Chicago, and Boston. Many are asking if the ranch is *420 friendly* [see glossary at end of book] or have cannabis-friendly lodging. The demographic seems to be mostly guys in their thirties and forties who are gainfully employed and enjoy all-inclusive packaging. There is a chef on site who prepares meals, and snacks are available all day long.

Ryan does have rules and regulations regarding activities and cannabis. For example, you cannot have consumed prior to riding ATVs or horses and skeet shooting. Fishing by the river is not allowed after consumption. The rules comply with state laws as well as some basic safety guidelines to keep the guests in a safe environment.

Ryan told me callers often seem a little apprehensive on the phone, but as soon as they pop the question about cannabis, they relax and begin sounding more at ease, even joking. At the bar, I hear lots of stories about difficulties out-of-state visitors have finding cannabis-friendly lodging, especially as many Homeowners' Associations don't allow cannabis in their condos.

My Two Favorite Head Shops

The first known use of a head shop was in the late sixties where drug paraphernalia like rolling papers, roach clips, hashish pipes, and bongs were sold in stores. Anyone remember those shops that had the lava lamps and black velvet, black light posters from the 1970s and 1980s? Well, they were probably head shops.

Head shops have come a long way since the black-velvet poster days. The art sold in them now is so creative and crafty it is worth taking a gander. Back in the day, hashish pipes were made mostly out of metal, woods, bamboo, brass, and some glass. Nowadays, crafting a pipe, or bowl as they are also known, involves glassblowing and intricate designs and colors.

I wanted to include two special head shops that I know about because of the wonderful characters who own them and work there, and the changes they have seen.

Smok N' Bra

Contact Information:
Ste-V Day
101 North Third Avenue
PO Box 2666
Frisco, Colorado 80443

www.SmokNBra.com
970-668-9665
(Open every day 11:00 a.m.–7:00 p.m.
18 years old and up)

Smok N' Bra, owned and operated by Ste-V Day, is actually more of an art gallery that also happens to sell paraphernalia, lingerie, and adult toys. So it's definitely one-stop shopping for a feisty evening! Everywhere you look in this shop there is something unique and fun. There are handmade T-shirts, bras, skate wear, skateboards, pipes, incense, artwork, paintings, and jewelry. Also in the store are handmade leather crafts, such as purses, dog collars, and armbands, some even decorated with stones from Colorado. And as far as body jewelry, Ste-V Day said she has enough to fill every possible piercing. She prides herself on selling art crafted in Colorado by local artists. She boasts the largest selection of body jewelry in Summit County.

"I started my business with four artists. I have over a hundred and sixty now. And growing! And the customers who come in, know they're getting a one-of-a-kind piece of art instead of just a tool," Ste-V Day says.

Always by her side, in the shop, is Odie, the sweetest and calmest pit bull.

Legalization has affected the way she stocks her store. Since the legalization of recreational marijuana to adults over twenty-one, the store began to focus more on smoking accessories, concentrate tools, and vaporizers. In addition to the many glass pipes, there are those made of antler, soapstone, alabaster rock, and wood. There are also specific pipes for marijuana oils and they are the hottest seller right now and growing. The adult section also has been growing due to more people wanting to have their weddings and party events in the mountains.

Summertime is fun at the store as artists sometimes set up glassblowing demonstrations out front on the deck. The glass art is something to be seen even if you don't partake in the toke culture; I saw a pipe in the store that had the coolest colors and the Colorado flag in the center of it. Sometimes Ste-V is asked to sell a disposable pipe, which she explains aren't disposable—they're art. If someone is going to go through the trouble of picking out a beautiful piece only to throw it away, it is better to give it away when finished. (The reason customers ask about disposable pipes is because once you smoke any cannabis in these pipes while in Colorado, a resin is left over, so you can't take a pipe you've used on a plane or out of the state).

The store is open to people eighteen years old and older. She doesn't want to change it to twenty-one because of all the art and jewelry that you don't need to be twenty-one to buy.

As we chatted away in the store, two gentlemen came in. They were travelling from Texas to Seattle, and they walked in with a smile from ear to ear. It was like watching two kids in a candy shop. I notice in a lot of places that people seem to be pretty mellow and happy when they are in the market for cannabis accessories.

The Fitter

Contact Information:
Bonnie and Betty
1303 Broadway Street
Boulder, CO 80302
http://TheFitterBoulder.com
info@TheFitterBoulder.com
303-442-4200

Bonnie and Betty, Hooka and Friends

It's the characters who own and operate these shops that make them special. This one is no different. The Fitter has been locally owned and operated in Boulder, Colorado, since 1973, originally called Pipefitter. It was one of the first full head shops in the Boulder area. Twin sisters, Betty and Bonnie bought the shop from their brother in 1975 for about $10,400 plus an initial investment of $5,000 (Bonnie, Betty, and their brother actually opened their first head shop in Phoenix, Arizona, in 1969, called The Inner Sanctum. The gals said they surely remember the black velvet poster and black light days. They even had a light room that they would switch on after hours. They called their friends to party it up, took the musical instruments off the wall, and played them to songs like "Light My Fire" by The Doors.

Some of the items they sold back then were water beds for $19.95, Nehru Jackets from the Beatles era, and pipes made of wood, plastic, and metal. The metal pipes were made from old lamp parts.

A big pipe room with a machine-gun turret in the middle had a sign that shoplifters would be shot. There was also a live hawk living in the store with his buddies, the boa constrictors.

The animal motif stayed with the siblings as they opened their Pipefitter store in Boulder in the early seventies. In the beginning years, the owners continued to enjoy having pet snakes roaming free in the Fitter. This sometimes led to interesting experiences in the store. Once, when Bonnie was working alone at the shop, their boa constrictor named Hooka somehow found its way into the interior mechanisms of the gigantic antique cash register they used for sales. The register locked up and wouldn't open. Nobody was able to remove the snake from the register or buy anything! Meanwhile, as this was all happening, the radio ad for The Fitter began to play on the radio over the speakers in the store. Bonnie says she will never forget because it was the ad that encouraged people to visit the shop and say "hi" to Hooka.

One snake disappeared in the store for six months. When the twins gave up hope and bought another snake, the missing snake appeared as if to say, "Oh, so you bought another snake, eh?" And it slithered straight up and out of a big skull pipe that was a giant glass centerpiece in the store.

The pet snakes would appear in the strangest places and scare the living hell out of customers. One snake hid in the rack of tapestries and showed up when a guy was looking through them. He screamed and ran for his life. Another favorite spot for the snakes was the big jewelry tree. They would hide in there and pop out when people were shopping for jewelry. The twins laughed as they told stories of people wearing the snakes around their necks and shoulders. Interesting times, those.

In the mid-eighties, the twins began fighting legal battles with the state of Colorado and the Federal Government. At the time it was illegal to sell drug paraphernalia. Betty and Bonnie felt that was wrong and unfair. If tobacco stores can sell pipes and gun stores sell guns, why couldn't they sell pipes? They weren't selling drugs.

"We were part of an association led by Denver attorney Arthur Schwartz that led the fight at the state level against paraphernalia laws," Betty said.

At the end of the 1980s, the women were delighted to finally get the call from the assistant district attorney congratulating them on winning the fight against the Colorado laws.

However, the federal battle was yet to be won. The twins continued to sell their products, since it was legal statewide, and the competition was already selling similar products. In 1991, their eighteen-year booming business run came to an abrupt end. Bonnie received a call on the morning of January 29, 1991, from her employee. "GET DOWN HERE NOW! THE FEDS ARE HERE!"

Betty heard about it and called the shop looking for

Bonnie. But federal agents answered the phone and would not get her. The feds had been staking out the shop for over a year in a sting operation called "Operation Pipe" in order to bust the illegal sale of drug paraphernalia.

The feds seized everything in the store. When Bonnie and Betty finally arrived at the shop, federal agents were taking inventory and boxing everything up. They took cash, inventory, files, mail, and froze all business and personal accounts. All told, the cost of fighting the federal raid in 1991, included the fine of $55,000, legal fees of $40,000, and inventory of $30,000, and totaled $125,000. It was in all the newspapers and news channels. They had to get three top attorneys to help them through these times. After eighteen years in business, they were about to start all over from scratch. Betty and Bonnie realized they couldn't win against the feds, so they agreed on a settlement. Had they fought and lost, there would have been mandatory jail time.

Bonnie recalls carrying around a lot of anger from the experience and feeling targeted because there were other head shops selling the same type of product that did not get raided. Finally, she decided to treat it as a simple business loss and changed her outlook on life. The two women applied for a new loan and began to rebuild as a gift shop with no paraphernalia. Bonnie's daughter, Erica, suggested selling girl's clothing and footwear at the Fitter and it took off again. Erica now owns a shop called Savvy selling these items and more just down the street in the Pearl Street Mall.

Although The Fitter bounced back from this setback, the sisters never stopped looking over their shoulders. They eventually phased in the pipes again, since all the shops in

Denver were already selling large quantities. They had to compete.

With the legalization of recreational marijuana on January 1, 2014, and a surge in pot tourism, the sisters threw a huge "Legalization Sale" and had a great month. It has since subsided after six months. When they opened up in 1973, they were the only game in town, with no competition. Now that weed is legal, they are feeling the squeeze from an over-saturation of head shops. Not to mention that the dispensaries also have display cases and are now selling paraphernalia as well. There are eight stores within eight blocks plus two new galleries that are now carrying glass pipes, bongs, and crafts. I hope these great women continue to thrive in spite of the crazy competitive environment in Colorado today.

The Ganja Kitchen Revolution: The Bible of Cannabis Cuisine

Contact Information:
Jessica Catalano
http://TGKR.co/

I had the pleasure of meeting Jessica Catalano, author of *The Ganja Kitchen Revolution*, at one of the Cultivating Spirits infused cooking seminars. Her 228-page illustrated cookbook makes me hungry and want to party at the same time. Her passion for cooking and her support of cannabis, especially in regard to pain management, shine through the pages. She is a pioneer of strain-specific cooking based on the pairing of flavor profiles of cannabis with recipes. This is the main key to her success along with an approachable style to cooking. She lives in Colorado, and the new laws have helped her find a wide variety of cannabis strains and elevate her recipes to a new level.

From the very first time she smoked weed, Jessica realized that it had a positive effect on her migraines. At the time, she didn't really understand why or how, but the cannabis had enabled her to function on a more productive level with the absence of migraines. One night, she observed a friend's mother making pot brownies, referring to the process as "making medicine." That little experience gave her the confidence, years later, to explore experimentation with cannabis infused edibles.

At Buffalo State in New York, she studied clinical psychology. From there she developed more of a general interest in medicine and transferred to EMT school. All the while she had a deep passion for cooking. She would cook all the time when friends would visit and beg her to cook more.

Eventually, Jessica found herself in Colorado, where she obtained her certification as an EMT. She worked for a time in a mental health detox center where the job was rewarding but something was missing. The internal nagging to become a chef and attend culinary school was always in the back of her mind, and she finally enrolled in Culinary School and graduated with a double major in Pastry Arts and Culinary Arts.

While in culinary school, she started cooking with cannabis. This is where the strain specific concept of edibles cooking was born. She began incorporating flavors of each strain into the recipes. Each strain, all plants for that matter, release terpenes, which are essential oils. Terpenes (or terpenoids) are responsible for the different smells and tastes of cannabis strains. For example, the strain of cannabis called Strawberry Cough has a strawberries, cream, and cedar aroma, so it works well as an ingredient in her recipe for strawberry shortcake. Jessica began blogging about cooking with cannabis in 2010. The original blog is found here: http://TheGanjaKitchenRevolution.blogspot.com/?m=1.

The new website which still produces free recipes just like the original is now here: www.TGKR.co simply titled The Ganja Kitchen Revolution.

The blog has basically moved to the new website and has been revamped.

Within just a few months, a publisher contacted her to write a cookbook. It took another three years of hard work, but the book was eventually published to acclaim by Green Candy Press. What a great success story.

Now Jessica writes for *Skunk Magazine*[9] as a food columnist, *Cannabis Now*[10] for recipes, *Ladybud Magazine Online*,[11] and occasionally *Releaf Magazine*.[12]

Aside from writing about cannabis as a career, Jessica is a chef for Cultivating Spirits Tour Company,[13] which offers responsible, educational, and spirited cannabis experiences in Summit County. (See page 31.)

At the end of this interview, I picked up my recorder and looked at the elapsed time and it was 34:20. I thought to myself that was a quick interview, and I showed it to Jessica to see if she thought the interview felt longer. The first thing she said was, "Oh, my God, it has 4:20 in it!" Lots of laughter ensued after that one.

Bud + Breakfast Lodging

Contact Information:

Silverthorne Location

Bud + Breakfast Silverthorne

Managers: Stephanie Colner and Michael Rocheleau

Address: 358 Lagoon Lane, Silverthorne, CO 80498

Phone: 970-368-6757

Hours: Open 24 hours daily. Check in is 4:00 p.m., check out is 11:00 a.m.

Email: MtnVista@BudandBfast.com

Room rates: $99–$249

Opened: October 2014

Denver Location
Bud + Breakfast at The Adagio
Owners: Joel and Lisa Schneider
Address: 1430 Race St., Denver, CO 80206
Phone: 303-370-6911
Hours: Open 24 hours daily. Check in 4:00 p.m.,
check out 11:00 a.m.
Email: info@BudandBfast.com
www.BudandBfast.com
Room rates: $249–$399
Opened: April 2014

Opened in 2014 in Silverthorne, Colorado, The Bud + Breakfast is a B&B owned by The MaryJane Group in Denver, Colorado, that caters to the cannabis enthusiast. According to its website (www.TheMaryJaneGrp.com): *"We are the first cannabis hospitality company to exist, and we now own the only two operating all-inclusive, cannabis-friendly lodges in the state of Colorado. There is no comparison: our rooms are the epitome of luxury, our food is delicious, our staff is attentive, and our top shelf samples are handpicked with care and scrutiny."*

Interview

Interviewer: Author
Interviewee: Stephanie Colner, manager
at Bud + Breakfast
Interview Setting: Bud + Breakfast Silverthorne Location

Johnny: Were there any special legal permits you needed to obtain? What was that process like?

Stephanie: Fortunately, we didn't need any special permits or licenses to start up the Bud + Breakfast, just your typical business license. According to Colorado law, it is legal to share or gift small amounts of cannabis to adults twenty-one years of age or older. We saw this as a great opportunity to share the buds of Colorado with our guests from around the country and the world. We require all of our guests to be twenty-one and provide state issued identification upon arrival.

Johnny: What was your inspiration for creating this concept?

Stephanie: Colorado currently allows in-state and out-of-state residents to purchase cannabis legally but does little to provide safe environments to consume it legally, much less socially. We wanted to provide a safe and comfortable place for out-of-state visitors and in-state residents to enjoy the products they legally purchased and paid taxes to the state of Colorado. Here, they are in a safe, controlled environment, and can enjoy it with really awesome people from somewhere else in the United States. It truly is a beautiful thing, and we get to meet and hang out with all of them. It's pretty awesome.

Johnny: How has business been?

Stephanie: Business has been fantastic! We love hearing from our guests how their dreams of a cannabis vacation have finally come true. Many have told us that they never thought they would see the day where they could stay in a beautiful mountain lodge that allowed the use of cannabis. The fact that we provide that very thing and have received overwhelmingly positive feedback from our guests, makes all the hard work we put into it worth it in every way.

Johnny: What has been the feedback from the community? Any supporters? Any protestors?

Stephanie: Over all, general feedback has been positive. Obviously, there are always going to be people who don't support cannabis. Therefore they don't support what we do. But for most people in Summit County and everywhere else, even those who don't partake, it's a really cool concept that allows people to safely consume cannabis in a social environment.

Johnny: What are your future plans? Expansion? Franchising?

Stephanie: We are trying to expand as much as possible in Colorado, Oregon, Washington, California. Wherever the wind takes us. However, first and foremost, we are the Bud + Breakfast brand. We want to uphold this standard—our concept of a clean, safe, cannabis haven for music lovers and stoners alike. So we have to find the right locations, the right employees, and the local law enforcement has to be willing to work with us, of course. Right now, our "Cannacamp" is in the works. I'm sure you will see a lot more about it in upcoming months in cannabis news. We have teamed up with Cultivating Spirits Cannabis Tour Company (See page 31), and have obtained a property with cabins that will provide water and electricity for a cannabis getaway stay in Durango. Essentially, it's an adult camp that will have cannabis-related activities as well as horseback riding, and so on. Twenty-one or over only.

Johnny: If there is anything you would like to say to the world about living in Colorado during the first year of legalization, what would it be?

Stephanie: It was the craziest, most exciting, most inspiring time of my life. Before the Bud + Breakfast, I needed direction. I had all of the tools to be successful, but Mike and I didn't have anything that we really loved doing that we could make a living off of. When we moved to Colorado in May of 2014 and I started working at the Adagio (our flagship location), it all came full circle. It has been a dream to wake up every day and witness all of these beautiful, young people of my generation take on this journey of showing the rest of the world how to legalize cannabis and how to do it right. I could go on and on about all of the good this entire industry has done for the state, the country . . . I mean, just ask our guests. We have been called pioneers countless times in the last ten months, and it is the best feeling in the world.

CHAPTER 5

Ganjapreneurial Products and Services

It took me a little over a month to chase down some of the busy dispensary owners. On my way to interview a dispensary owner, Rhett Jordan of Native Roots, I discovered an opportunity for an impromptu interview with an event planner who has expanded into cannabis events.

It was a nice surprise when I arrived to see Rhett in a meeting with event planner Freddie Wyatt, CEO of Munch & Co. Freddie joined in our discussion. He talked about the early 1990s in Aspen when it was a haven for Hollywood producers, actors, and the rich and famous. Freddie, Jordan, and I had lunch at Mezzaluna, which according to Wyatt, was the hot spot for après ski (happy hour after skiing) back in the day. The likes of Donald Trump, Vannah White, Kirk Douglas, and MTV gals were seen there frequently.

Freddie was in Aspen to prepare for a big event during the 2015 X-Games. Hired by Native Roots, they threw a VIP cannabis-friendly event at the Crystal Palace, complete with indoor trees and tree houses, that included the likes of DJ Snoopadelic (Snoop Dogg), Wiz Khalifa and DJ Bonics, Griz, Michal Menert, TJ Mizell, Manic Focus, Lily Fangz, Adventurous, DJ Mark Frank Montoya, and Congo Sanchez of Thievery Corporation to name a few. Munch, which is a Denver-based, nationwide activation company, specializes in strategic marketing/branding and event production.

Their website states the following: "Last year, Native Roots Colorado and Munch & Co. were able to create and execute an unbelievable social experience in beautiful Aspen, Colorado. Showcased during the winter X Games, the now legendary iRecreate House provided a safe oasis for guests to gather and celebrate. Visited by over two thousand people—professional athletes, famous personalities, thought leaders, socialites, locals, and X Games patrons—spanning a four-day period, the iRecreate house was able to successfully achieve another landmark event."[14]

Pot Vending Machines

Lots of folks at the bar have been talking to me about pot vending machines. I think they are a really innovative invention, but I'm not so sure pot should be quite so easy to buy. I wouldn't support a vodka vending machine either. But be that as it may, pot vending machines have been going through many prototypes and trials over the past few years and several have made the cut. Using biometrics to validate age and medical cards, these machines are being slowly introduced on a trial basis so as to monitor efficiency and usage issues.

A machine called the ZaZZZ, which was displayed at a restaurant in Avon, Colorado, "uses biometrics to verify a customer's age. The machine is climate-controlled to keep its product fresh," according to an article on www.NPR.org, and was created by a company called American Green for medical patients only.[15]

THC Infused Sexual Stimulant

That's correct: customers at my bars told me about marijuana-based sex lubes that claim to increase the intensity of orgasms. I saw one myself, in stores, called "Floria." It is a mixture of cannabis and coconut oil that you can grease up on yourself and your partner—and supposedly it works better for women than men.

420 Friendly Accommodations

When referring to lodging, "420" means that it is okay to possess and smoke recreational marijuana on the property. Colorado law permits the owners of hotels and private rentals to make their own policy regarding smoking on premises. It is a big question these days when inquiring about accommodations. People want to know if they are going to be safe and legal when it comes to partaking in the new industry. Many hotels and lodgings are 420 friendly. A simple internet search will help you find all the 420 friendlies you need. It is still a new business model, and many providers are still defining terms and policies. So it looks like marijuana tourism is real, and it is alive and well out here in Colorado.

Marijuana Questionnaires

Some companies that sell consumable cannabis products are putting out questionnaires to gauge your experience level with marijuana so they know what strain to recommend and how many milligrams of THC. A company called Dixie Elixirs and Edibles in Denver, Colorado, has a fantastic index card that incorporates a scoring system based on your prior experience with marijuana. Depending on your experience with edibles, body weight, and personality type, you are assigned total points. Based on those points, they can recommend specific products and the amount of milligrams. Their products range from THC infused massage oils, bath soaks, one-dose mints, one-dose coconut water, one-dose chocolates, and a variety of flavored sodas. The company also has a fantastic Marijuana 101 booklet that walks you through the process of either consuming or refraining from marijuana. Dixie Elixirs is part of MJNA stock listed in our pot stocks chapter. For more information and current index cards go to www.DixieElixirs.com.

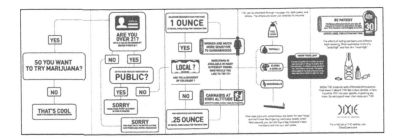

CHAPTER 6

The Buyers, Consumers, and Traders of Cannabis

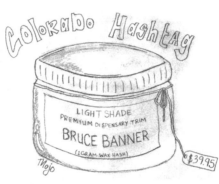

Illustration by Mariah Hildreth

A Johnny Bartender Observation

What amazed me most when pot was first legalized was the type of person who comes into the restaurants where I work and asks me about the new industry. I would have guessed folks interested in pot would mostly have been younger, ragged-looking snowboarders and skateboarder types. Instead, much of the time it is the soft spoken older, well-to-do, retired community that is seeking advice. Whether old or young, almost everyone asking me about pot is well-spoken, direct, and polite.

No Permission Slip for You, Sir

A close personal friend told me a story about his experience with his bank and trying to apply for his medical marijuana card. In order to apply for your medical marijuana card, there is a list of documents and forms needed along with the necessary paperwork from a physician. One of these documents needs to be signed in front of a notary public. My friend went to his bank to have this done. He has been a client of this bank for over twelve years with all his personal and business banking. He is retired now, but his business was a very successful one allowing him to retire comfortably. When he went in to sign the document in front of the bank's notary public, they refused to notarize the document from a licensed physician because it dealt with marijuana. There is still a fair amount of concern over federal laws and the Federal Reserve that rules the banks, as marijuana is still illegal federally.

The Town Stoner: A Non-Interview

I really wanted to get some great stories for you from our local "Town Stoner." I really tried. It's just that when you hang out with the Town Stoner things don't tend to stay very . . . linear.

Let me backtrack. Most towns have that one guy who everyone knows or assumes is always high on weed. Our town is no different, except we have several. The one I chose to interview is a good friend, and it just happens that his actual house address is—believe it or not—420 [See Glossary for 420 reference]. That is no joke. He has been there for over fourteen years. People have been known to light up joints near this address because of its popularity in stoner culture.

"The Town Stoner"

Illustration by Ryan Spencer

What qualifies this friend (I'll call him "TS") to be considered for the prestigious "Town Stoner" title? For starters, TS likes to smoke a lot of pot. There may even have been some selling of weed in the past. By the past, I mean it was at least seven years ago. On top of the enjoyment of cannabis products, this guy goes to as many music shows, festivals, and hippie retreats as are scheduled here in the mountains. He can usually be found near the front row spinning or twirling around in the typical stoner dance moves. Some of his moves are so stealthy. He has had success by leaving his backpack in the front row hours before a show would start and then finagling his way back in later.

In addition to his concert habits, he has skied some of the most dangerous mountains in Colorado and was filmed for a ski video at one time. TS has worked in the ski industry for over sixteen years, doing everything from checking ski lift tickets to fitting ski boots.

The following anecdote may give you a sense of my friend TS. In 2004 he was arrested in California for possession. He used his one phone call to call a bar in Frisco, the Moose Jaw. The Jaw was the one place he knew someone would answer his call. Sure enough, they bailed him out. While waiting for the bail to post, he smoked pot in jail.

He has also planted an American flag on top of Peak One Mountain after the September 11 attack, gone on tour with The Grateful Dead, and driven a 1977 Chevy van from the United States to the southernmost tip of South America, going through Mexico and Central America. He's notorious for leaving a trail of open bar tabs at the many watering holes across town. TS is the only person I know who can go barhopping on Main Street with no money in his pocket and come home wasted several nights in a row.

I interviewed him informally for this book on October 1, 2014. We were already getting snow up here in the mountains, so we decided to meet indoors—where else but at the 420 address? When I showed up, a mutual friend was already there with TS. I showed them all the work I had done for the book so far and got ready to ask my questions.

I began by asking what changes he has noticed up here in the mountains since the legalization of recreational marijuana. He said there really isn't much of a change except that the tourists are more interested. I could tell by his response that the question and answer routine wasn't flowing. I told the guys to relax and grab a beer and let's hang out like we normally do. Oh, and I almost forgot, they had already rolled a joint that looked like a baby's arm holding an apple.

So the guys grabbed cans of beer out of the little mini fridge. The beers were just a little too cold and had begun to freeze, so they poured some out into mugs. Then they set the open beer cans behind us on the counter. As we continued the "interview," the big joint was lit and passed around. I refrained, but it didn't matter. I got hot boxed anyway. ("Hot boxed" is synonymous with getting a contact high or high by proximity.) In the middle of a sentence, TS heard something dripping behind him.

"What the hell is that noise? Do you hear it?"

Drip. Drip. Drip.

It was one of the iced-up beer cans that had expanded after twenty minutes, spilled on the counter, and was now dripping on the carpet. That caused a thunderous uproar of laughter from us all and set the tone for the rest of the interview.

Next, TS handed me a copy of *The Grateful Dead; The Illustrated Trip*[16], and told me how cool it is. Then he showed me his Sunshine Daydream Journal, also very cool, and began to write today's entry in it.

"October 1st: interview with Johnny Welsh for *The Pot Chronicles: Year One* . . . ha ha ha." Again, we all burst out laughing. I'm still not sure why.

The conversation drifted around from the eighteen inches of snow Silverton, Colorado, received the day before to being cut off from drinking on airplanes. A friend of TS was concerned he wouldn't make it through security on a recent flight from San Francisco.

Then, as if awakening from a trance, TS said, "Oh yeah, and the quality of the pot has gotten better since January first and street prices have gone down."

That was pretty much the whole interview. We began to make plans for the next time we would all hang out, and that conversation degenerated into a discussion about which bars we each had been to in the previous seventy-two hours.

I'd say it was a great success. What else would you expect when you try to interview the Town Stoner?

Weed as Gratuity: It's Green like Currency!

There have been many times in the past when I have received marijuana instead of cash tips, as a bartender, from those who have bought cannabis and cannot bring it back home (out of state) with them. This happens a lot in the restaurant industry but also in an industry that is special to the Rocky Mountains. Here is a story from my friend Karpy (Stephen Karp), a ski instructor from a nearby ski resort.

Weedy Gratuity

Now that marijuana is legal in Colorado, it's in the news just about every day. I don't smoke pot. Ganja isn't part of my life. It is part of mountain resort life and the food and beverage industry where I also work. And, as we all know, nobody parties in the restaurant biz. *Right.* Wacky tobacky drifts around me, friends get high, folks ask about where to buy hooch, but I never thought much about reefer. Boooommm! Weed is legal after seventy-five years of prohibition. I still don't know where to buy Sticky Icky, but it's unavoidable.

A wonderful group of people from the Midwest booked me as their ski instructor for three glorious days. Let's call them "The Davenports." After meeting for a nice breakfast, our adventure began. Six hours later, day one is under our belts, followed by an evening of a few beers and glory stories of the day.

Remember I don't get high, barely drink, and have tried cannabis maybe four times in my entire life. The years have snuck up on me now, and back when I did try it, it was schwag, meaning weak weed. As I walked with the group after skiing, I was suddenly aware of a sweet smell of cannabis. Ninety-nine percent of the time if someone asked if I wanted a hit, I would have thanked the person and waved it off. But these people are good clients, bill payers, lunch buyers, and really nice people. In the corner of my eye, I see the joint getting closer and closer, the scent warning me that it's almost my turn. What will I do? Anxiety set in. If it wasn't legal, there was no question for me: thanks, but no thanks. I just didn't get high. Now it's legal. Now it's showtime for Karpy. What can one or two hits do? It'll be fine. Well, I missed that night's meeting. Fast-food wrappers littered my kitchen, and my face muscles really hurt the next morning from laughing and smiling.

We skied together for the next two days. Great times, great weather, wonderful snow, and Colorado and Copper Mountain skiing lived up to their reputations. Business cards were swapped. The group leader shook my hand with a concealed ample tip for the effort. After hugs and more hand-shakes from all, it was time to take my leave. I heard, "Hey, Karpy. Here's one more little something to express our gratitude for your time with us." And there, like a little Christmas present dressed perfectly in beautiful wrapping paper, was my first ever assortment of cannabis edibles and three different vials of the Devil's Lettuce (cannabis wax extracts).

Surprised, and in uniform, on Resort property I didn't know what to do. People leave gifts at guest services all the time for ski instructors after a good ski lesson. I am not used to receiving such gifts in front of 200 skiers in front of the main lodge. There it was, gift-wrapped laughing grass. It was awkward, but very cool and so 2014. Now what do I do with it? It is still illegal to have at Copper as an employee, let alone at Copper in uniform in front of the world. Suddenly, I'm rubbernecking, looking for the law, coworkers, and known management. I thought for sure I was going to get busted. So without the Davenports seeing, I found a secret hiding place and stuffed the gift there.

I changed out of uniform, returned to the scene, retrieved my beautiful gift bag, and whiffed the same scent that wiped out an entire evening of my life the day before. Can I have it on me? Can it be in my car? What the hell am I going to do with it?

That night, the team that I work with at the restaurant got an unexpected snack and smoke for later that night. The vials were labeled with flowery names, and the edibles had chocolate, oatmeal, sugar, cinnamon, and the tasty treats I enjoyed. Needless to say, my friends at the restaurant didn't get all of them. And yes, my face hurt the next day again. Another trail of food wrappers covered the living room, the TV was on, I had one shoe off, my coat still on, and a half-eaten oatmeal flowery sensation bar was in my hand.

I wish there was a moral to my story, but there isn't. It's just a "unique to Colorado" story that I will remember forever. As for the group from the Midwest, hats off and thank you. To those coming to Colorado and enjoying any of its recreational bounty, including the almost infinite strains of marijuana, enjoy, be smart, don't try to take over the state border, and know where fast-food restaurants are located beforehand.

CHAPTER 7

Budtenders: Sellers on the Front Lines

There are many tales to tell from the "high country." Some of the ones I found most intriguing came from people who make their living selling cannabis. If you're considering entering this industry, you might find a few nuggets (pun intended) of wisdom. Enjoy the interviews, as these are the true stories that don't often show up in mainstream media.

The Life of a Budtender

Budtender, n. *A person who is similar to a bartender selling alcohol. Budtenders sell marijuana buds or flower. Like bartenders, they are responsible for checking identification and age verification. They can usually be spotted a mile away by their smile from ear to ear, their eagerness to chat, and their excessive happiness due to having a career in cannabis.*

There are budtender universities and budtender college sites all over the Internet. I even found a budtender résumé template online! Retail sales jobs in the cannabis industry require what is known as a "support badge." This allows you to sell recreational marijuana. Here are just a few requirements to obtaining the budtender support badge in Colorado.

1. Applicants must be 21 years of age or older.

2. Applicants may not have any controlled substance felony convictions.

3. Applicants may not have any other felony convictions that have not been fully discharged five years prior to applying.

4. Applicants may not have any delinquent government or child support debt.

5. Applicants may not be a sheriff, deputy sheriff, police officer, prosecuting officer, or an employee of the state or local licensing authority.

6. Applicants must be Colorado residents at the time of application.

There is also a fee involved with obtaining this support badge. As of this writing, the fee is $150, but I have a feeling that this well be forever changing (most likely increasing).[17]

The actual training to become a budtender is very specific to the university, and different dispensaries have different educational requirements for their budtenders. Most courses include homework covering the different strains of cannabis. Budtenders receive homework once a week in the form of two grams of different strains of flower to analyze. Most dispensaries have some type of training program. Not all are the same, however.

Interview with a Manager/Budtender

Contact Information:
Andrew Benton
861 North Summit Blvd,
Frisco, CO 80443
www.NativeRoots303.com
NativeRootsSummit@gmail.com
970-368-6024

Andrew Benton, budtender-turned-dispensary-manager, stopped into the bar for some dinner one evening, and I quickly seized the opportunity to ask a few questions regarding his experiences. Born and raised in Colorado, Andrew grew up with the view of Red Rocks Amphitheatre right from his backyard. His experience in the marijuana industry dates back through nine years of personal interest and study with the last ten months in the recreational industry. In that time, Andrew started out as a budtender and is currently the manager of a dispensary. This is a rather fast timeframe for such advancement, and it goes to show how rapidly the industry has grown since legalization.

Andrew had quite a bit of fun as he shared with me some of the new terminology and jargon associated with this fledgling industry. Here are a few of those terms.

Budtender Phraseology

1. In order to help tell the difference between *indica* and *sativa*, the phrase is, "Sunny *Sativa* vs. *Indica* In-da-couch," meaning that *sativa* is more of an uplifting functional high and *indica* being more of a body relaxer.

2. "Pep in your step" means the product will give you energy.

3. "Zombie couch lock" means what it sounds like.

4. With edibles, always start low and slow. You can always eat more, but it's much harder to un-eat them.

For more of these expressions, see the Glossary at the back of this book.

The most intriguing aspect of his work is the difference between the medical side and recreational side of marijuana sales. The reason the word *"side"* applies to the division between marijuana sales, both figuratively and literally, is medical marijuana is on the other side of a wall from recreational marijuana, even if both are sold under one roof in a dispensary. Each must be sold in a separate room. Medical patients are very specific as to what their needs are. The recreational side sees a lot of first timers.

Andrew says that it is fun to watch the first timers as they come in and are initially a little timid about asking questions. After a few minutes, when they are treated with extreme professionalism by the staff, they begin to relax and realize it is a legitimate business with a very real potential to help. The budtenders call it going from "a deer in the headlights" to "a kid in a candy store." They say it is fun to watch this evolution take place. Most newcomers are shocked at the level of professionalism at dispensaries.

After the initial awkwardness is resolved, budtenders explain to the recreational customers the various benefits of the products. Once the customers are relaxed, they learn a lot about extractions, topicals, edibles, and the flower itself. The "rec" side has become a platform to illustrate the many uses of the plant. Customers on the recreational side usually know what they want the marijuana to do for them. They describe how they want to feel and based on that the budtender makes a recommendation. Customers may say things like, "I don't want to be sleepy," "I don't like feeling paranoid," "I don't want to feel jittery," or "I want to feel alert and happy." There is a specific bud for every person, and finding that type is the budtender's job.

Homework for a Budtender from Native Roots

Directions: *After consuming a strain, please report and rate how it makes you feel. Please analyze and critique the flower as from the position of a cannasseur.*

Name/Contact:
Strain:
Method of Ingestion:
Context/Setting/Activity:
Taste/Smell/Description:
Feelings/Reactions:
Rate: (1 lowest to 5 highest)

On a scale from 1–5, how happy does this make you feel?

1 2 3 4 5

On a scale from 1–5, how energized does this strain make you feel?

1 2 3 4 5

On a scale from 1–5, how tired does this strain make you feel?

1 2 3 4 5

On a scale from 1–5, how functional would you rate this strain?

1 2 3 4 5

On a scale from 1–5, how strongly would you recommend this strain to an inexperienced smoker?

1 2 3 4 5

In your opinion, rate this strain according to *sativa*, *indica*, or hybrid.
(1 being *sativa*, 2–4 hybrids, and 5 being *indica*)

1 2 3 4 5

Budtenders are the face of the industry. They are on the front lines and they have the power to change the viewpoint of marijuana within the general public's eye. At the same time, they are outcasts, constantly smelling of the product, receiving judging stares, and turned up noses from people passing by. Knowledge is the budtender's main weapon to change the view towards marijuana and the growing industry. It's become so much more than just "getting high," and it's our job to show the world what this industry is truly about.

—Andrew Benton, Manager of Native Roots

Dispensaries: Pot Shops and Their Owners

"Earlier this week—this is crazy—the country's first
marijuana cafe opened up, which not only sells medical
marijuana, but also has a restaurant where customers
can eat. In a related story, the recession is over."
—Conan O'Brien, *The Tonight Show with Conan O'Brien*,
November 2009

I visited some dispensaries in Colorado to get the full story from the people who ran them and to see for myself what was really happening. My first visit was to a dispensary located directly across from the Denver Broncos' football stadium in a very urban part of Denver.

Tru Cannabis Mile High

Contact Information:
Justin Staley
Tru Cannabis Mile High
1705 Federal Blvd.
Denver, CO 80204
http://MHMCDenver.com
303-455-9333

As I walked up to this dispensary, I noticed two entrances: one for medical marijuana, for people ages eighteen and over who had been issued Medical Marijuana Cards, and the other for recreational marijuana, restricted to people ages twenty-one and over.

One of the partners, Justin Staley, agreed to an interview with me, even with his busy schedule. This guy works non-stop. He runs three stores in the Denver area. I was impressed with his enthusiasm and knowledge of the industry, especially of the legalities and current events.

Interview

Interviewer: Author
Interviewee: Justin Staley
Interview Setting: Tru Cannabis Mile High formerly Mile High Recreational Cannabis

Johnny: Approximately how many people come through your doors per day? Per week?

Justin: Well, we have two sides to our store. On the medicinal use side, we see about 230 customers per week. On the recreational side, we see about 250 customers per day.

Johnny: Have you had lines of customers out the door?

Justin: Yes, we have had lines wrapping around the building. I thought it would subside quickly, but even a few months after opening we were twenty deep per day. That is why we hired security personnel. We are right across from the Bronco football stadium, Invesco Field. During the playoffs in 2014 about 30 percent of our customers were New England Patriots fans.

Johnny: What percent of your customers generally would you guess to be from out of state?

Justin: About 40 percent are from out of state and 10 percent are international customers.

Johnny: Any issues like running out of product?

Justin: Yes, we had to buy additional product from our partners in our network of affiliate stores.

Johnny: How many jobs has your store created?

Justin: We currently have eighteen employees.

Johnny: Have there been any protests or opposition?

Justin: No, there hasn't.

Johnny: What's the worst story you can think of?

Justin: We did have a theft. Someone broke in looking for valuables. We watched them on the surveillance cameras the next day. They seemed to be on some heavy drugs.

Johnny: Any worries about the Feds?

Justin: No, not in Colorado. They do need to give the banks the go ahead.

Johnny: Have any other states contacted you about advice for their legislation?

Justin: Yes, the state of Massachusetts Department of Health did a walk-through and wanted consulting but didn't have the backing.

Johnny: Have your numbers exceeded expectations?

Justin: Yes.

Johnny: How do you feel about the illegal dealers that are still out there?

Justin: They are shrinking. We even noticed a gang member who came in to buy retail recreational—probably because his suppliers are drying up.

Johnny: What industry/career were you in prior to this?

Justin: Licensed in property and casualty insurance sales.

Johnny: Down the road there might be more pressure to prevent underage consumption. Any ideas around this?

Justin: The selling of medicinal marijuana, which has been here for three years, has already required childproof and locking packages, so we have already been doing that. It is now more in the public mind because recreational is legal, but those measures have already been in place to limit exposure to children and pets.

Johnny: What are your plans for growth and expansion?

Justin: Buy licenses here locally and take over struggling shops. Sometimes we look at other states, but why leave right now?

Johnny: In a nutshell—since the whole world wants to know—how is it going?

Justin: Better than expected. The police have been so supportive. They are asking us how best to help and serve with this new industry.

Herbal Bliss

Contact Information:
Dawn Mlatecek
842 North Summit Blvd,
Frisco, Colorado 80443
HerbalBliss.wix.com/Herbal-Bliss
BHCFrisco@gmail.com
970-668-3514

Dawn Mlatecek spoke freely and eloquently about her experience in this business. Her store, located in a ski resort town, is very different from the Tru Cannabis Mile High in Denver.

Birthday Margaritas

We started out with a couple of margaritas to celebrate Dawn's birthday and the interview. She immediately broke into a funny story about one of the store's first customers. On opening day, a hippie in his mid-sixties, sporting a big grey beard, came into the store just glowing with a smile from ear to ear. After shopping around and smelling the different jars of the many strains of recreational marijuana, he asked if he could take some photos, then he asked the staff to take a picture of him holding up his new purchase of a bag of weed. He immediately texted the pictures to his buddy, who had spent seven years in prison for marijuana-related charges.

At the end of his visit, his excitement barely in check, he took one final photo at the store's exit to commemorate the unbelievable—to him—fact that yes, he had purchased marijuana and yes, had actually left the store without incident.

Dawn's History

Dawn has quite the business and entrepreneurial background. She graduated from Johnson & Wales University and began working in restaurants and doing some consulting. When she realized that she didn't enjoy working for others, she went off on her own and purchased a single Schlotzsky's Deli franchise. Over the next five years, she also helped other franchisees open up dozens of these stores across the nation.

She visited many states, fell in love with Colorado, and eventually sold off her franchise and moved here.

After some business development consulting, she went back to school to study naturopathy. I am impressed and amazed at the work she does with allergy and pain elimination through energy rebalancing.

Her franchise knowledge combined with her passion for alternative healing make her a natural fit as a pioneer in the marijuana dispensary business.

Interview

Interviewer: Author
Interviewee: Dawn Mlatecek
Interview Setting: Hacienda Real Restaurant, Frisco, CO

Johnny: Approximately how many people come through your store per week?

Dawn: Seven hundred to a thousand per week.

Johnny: What percent would you guess to be out-of-state customers?

Dawn: In the beginning, in January, it was about 85–90 percent out-of-state customers. Now it has pulled back a little to be closer to 70 percent out of state.

Cannabis Customers

Dawn told me about a woman who came to see Dawn after trying dozens of Western medical treatments to help with her fibromyalgia. It worked—the next time the woman saw Dawn, she said she hadn't felt that good in years.

Dawn's customer base cuts widely across the demographic spectrum. She gets a lot of sixty- to seventy-year-olds who have never tried marijuana. Some of these folks ask for strains that can help with sex drive. On the other end of the age range are the college kids coming to town for spring break. Dawn said she has been blown away by how polite and responsible they are. They only purchase just enough to consume while they are here for their stay and do not overdo it.

There are always a few people who ask how to take some out of Colorado to which Dawn responds firmly, "You can't. It's illegal to cross state lines with marijuana."

(Interview continued)

Johnny: How many jobs has your store created?

Dawn: Ten.

Johnny: Have you had any issues like running out of product?

Dawn: Nope.

Parking Lot Sales?

Dawn broke into another story about a crazy man who was trying to sell his own bags of weed in the parking lot of her dispensary. It was during the first month of business. Some guy in his fifties decided to set up shop and sell marijuana illegally to people on their way to the dispensary. Not one person purchased from this guy, and he became agitated. He entered the store and began shouting, "You are all damned! You are all going to hell! You are giving money to 'the man'!" Dawn and her staff called the police and they promptly removed him.

Toward the end of our lunch interview, Dawn joked about which states she figured would be last to legalize pot: Utah, Nebraska, Kansas, Oklahoma, and Texas.

The crazy thing about her list is that the day before I interviewed Dawn, Utah had just passed a measure allowing for limited medical use of marijuana. You just never know.

Last, we talked about some of the negatives in the industry. Dawn felt that the illegal dealers should be completely shut down, even some of the caregivers who grow marijuana for patients with medical cards. Some unscrupulous caregivers have had their friends get cards, so they could have the caregiver grow one hundred plants legally for them. She told me that not all caregivers are doing this, but there are some bad apples in the bunch who could potentially spoil things for those who are following all the laws and rules.

High Country Healing

HIGH COUNTRY HEALING

Contact Information:
Nick Brown
191 Blue River PKWY #202
Silverthorne, Colorado 80498
www.HighCountryHealing.com
970-468-7858

I love Nick Brown's story: An Ivy League graduate does very well for himself then loses it all and starts over from scratch. Embarking on a new business in a fresh and unique industry, he rises to the top again, overcoming constant changes in laws, rules, and regulations.

Nick Brown owns a dispensary in Silverthorne, Colorado, and part of one in Alma, Colorado, which is probably the highest elevation dispensary in the country. Both dispensaries include medical and recreational sales. He also has a partnership in three stores in Colorado Springs and owns a total of four grow facilities with more on the way. He started with $51,000 and a small operation, is now debt free, and has generated millions of dollars in sales.

Now this gentleman is impressive. Only in his early thirties, he has a business mind that I would put up against any business mind out there. The amount of legal knowledge, understanding of inventory, tracking, pricing, growing, and customer service that Nick possesses would be impressive even to the top anti-marijuana proponent.

Once again, my head is spinning at how big this industry is and how many businesses can be created. I feel a little like Napoleon Hill interviewing so many highly successful individuals and learning a little bit of the mindset. This book could easily be titled *Think and Grow Weed or Grow Weed and Grow Rich*.

Nick's History

High school football player of the year plus straight A's landed Nick admission to Princeton University, where he played free safety on the team all four years.

Being from Colorado originally, it was hard to give up the mountain vistas and the mountain life, so he came back to his home state to work in the real estate industry with his dad. The father and son team took a lending company from $28 million in loans to $80 million from 2005 to 2007 and were doing quite well. Then in 2008, when things were bad for most of the planet, the Browns were equally devastated, and they lost everything, including their private jet.

After selling real estate in Breckenridge, Colorado, from 2008 to 2009, Nick began paying closer attention to the movement to legalize medical marijuana. He sensed the tide changing and put himself in a position to be ready to obtain a license for a dispensary as soon as the law passed. As an advocate of weed, he immediately scraped up $51,000 and found his location in Silverthorne.

Yes, Nick is one of those people who saw the opportunity when it first surfaced.

When he filed for his application for the state license to sell medical marijuana, officials at the town hall said that they had never seen any business like this filed before. They saw no reason not to accept the application. It was approved. The next day the newspapers went wild with the big weed story, and the town placed a moratorium on future licenses for medical marijuana. High Country Healing became the second medical dispensary to open in Summit County.

The Backpack Years

At first, Nick acquired houses in which to grow product for the stores. Then a law was passed requiring more licensing, and it was not possible to license houses for growth, so that plan was done. This triggered the "backpack sellers."

The year 2010 was the Wild, Wild West of the backpack years, when caregivers would show up and sell pot out of their backpacks to the dispensaries.

Soon more laws were passed to outlaw the backpackers and require them to be licensed growers *for* a dispensary, and only the *dispensary* could license them. The next logical step would be to learn how to build grow facilities, which is just what Nick did. This really ramped up production. Nick chose two growers and basically said, "Show me what you can do." He still has one of these growers today and will put him up against any grower on the planet. This grower is one with the plant. He knows from seed to sale the best care to give the plants for the best and highest quality yield. Using soil only— no hydroponics, and all organic—he tends to them like eggs in a nest.

Recreational Marijuana Legalized

It was nearly impossible to jump through all the hoops required in order to have your doors open on the morning of January 1, 2014, when recreational stores officially became legal to run. As Brown explained, before the store could open, all plants and inventory had to be tagged with radio frequency ID tags, now called METRC Marijuana Inventory Tracking Solutions. But only one company sold the METRC tags in those days. Order and delivery was supposed to take three days. Nick hedged his bet and placed his order three weeks prior to January 1, so that they would have ample time to tag and inventory everything they had for recreational sale.

The shipping was delayed. The tags showed up on December 31. While the rest of us were celebrating New Year's Eve, Nick and his staff spent the night tagging weed until 4:00 a.m. They made it happen.

When January 1 dawned, Nick owned two of the thirty-two recreational stores in Colorado that were ready to open their doors. In Silverthorne, there was a line of people down two flights of stairs and out into the parking lot. At 10:00 a.m. when they opened their doors, fifty people came barreling in, and they were happy to wait the thirty minutes it took to get what they wanted. Everyone was hugging and high fiving and there was a total of ZERO problems. "It was a sight to be seen," Nick says.

I know from my work in restaurants that it takes a certain finesse to greet and seat customers, get them what they want, and then go on to the next customer. I can't even imagine being a budtender during those early days of legalization. They got so many people out for their first time ever in a dispensary or who had never tried cannabis and needed to be educated on responsible consumption.

Today, it is more difficult to get a license to open a store. The local jurisdictions have absolute power on whether to ban it, allow it, or allow some of it.

Wise Cooperation with the Law

Nick invited the town council and the police force into his Silverthorne shop before the big opening day. He explained to them everything from top to bottom, including what to expect, during a laid-back educational tour. He forged a positive relationship with the town, which helped facilitate a quick resolution of any problem. For example, they faced one problem when the smell of the plants of the grow facility became too strong. Nick talked with the town council and police and rectified the problem with a $50,000 filtration system. No shutdowns, no animosity. There is an amazing open communication between Nick and the town that doesn't exist in some families that I know.

Budtenders and staff members at Nick's dispensaries hand out an index card with each purchase on which are printed rules and regulations. This is a voluntary action that Nick created with help from local law enforcement.

Nick was featured on November 30, 2014, on an MSNBC special called "Pot Barons of Colorado," which also interviewed many other dispensaries and businesses.

Nick Brown's Handout with Purchase

- Customer must be 21 years of age or older to purchase, possess, or consume recreational marijuana.
- Open consumption (smoking, inhaling, or edibles) is not allowed in public, on public lands, streets, sidewalks, parking lots, common areas, or public buildings.
- Consumption of marijuana may be allowed in private locations, such as a residence, providing it is not prohibited by the property owner.
- Consumption of marijuana in a vehicle is not allowed and driving under the influence of marijuana is illegal.
- Selling marijuana to another person or transporting to another state is illegal.

At the Shops

Nick's phone messages and e-mails are filled with the résumés of aspiring budtenders from all walks of life. One applicant had a degree in microbiology, a minor in math, and a certificate in finance and wanted nothing more than to be a budtender. Yes, it is safe to say that it is raining résumés in Colorado.

When I toured the Silverthorne dispensary, I was again impressed with the staff and their ability to spend time with customers, giving them each delicate personal attention.

The computer registers are operated on a software system known as Biotrack, which tracks plants from seed to sale and handles inventory. At the time of our interview, Nick said that the latest software was still not fast or diverse enough to handle the volume or creative sales tactics, such as happy-hour price changes.

When Silverthorne opened, it held ten employees; the number quickly jumped to twenty-five. Now, they have created over forty jobs—and climbing—in the mountains of Colorado.

Nick and I agreed that there is tremendous advantage to being first in an industry. Is it possible that guys with the names like Carnegie, Ford, Rockefeller, and Gates stood upon a similar precipice at one point in time?

Nick, to me, embodies success as one of my favorite authors Timothy Ferriss describes it:

I'm often asked how I define "success." It's an overused term, but I fundamentally view this elusive beast as a combination of two things—achievement and appreciation. One isn't enough. Achievement without appreciation makes you ambitious but miserable. Appreciation without achievement makes you unambitious but happy.[18]

Medical Marijuana of the Rockies

"Creating a Community of Healing through Sharing, Knowledge, and Love."

Contact Information:
Jerry Olson
(Store Closed)
www.MMRockies.com (website still active)

Have a seat at the bar. This is a story of a once-thriving dispensary that is now closed. But, who knows, with our help MMR may rise again.

I have met dispensary owners who have great business minds and visions of mega profits. I have also met those who are true believers in the healing power of cannabis. Jerry Olson is one of those believers. He has an authentic passion for spreading the word and helping those who suffer feel better. He genuinely believes it is a birthright for everyone in this world to be able to have access to a plant he is convinced will help so many who may be suffering unnecessary pain and illness.

Jerry was a Colorado trailblazer, one of the first to open a dispensary. Here's what led him to become one of the leading proponents of cannabis in healing.

While a college student in 1990, he had ulcerative colitis and became so sick that he lost fifty pounds in one month. He was administered massive doses of steroids to try to get the inflammation down, but it didn't work. Parts of his infected colon were removed, and the steroids themselves caused steroid-induced diabetes. At the same time, it was discovered that he also had primary sclerosing cholangitis of the liver and would need a liver transplant later in life.

After the operation on Jerry's colon, he began experimenting with different strains of cannabis for pain management. He made a surprising discovery. Most college-aged young adults who consumed cannabis would get a relaxed feeling or become lethargic. For Jerry, the effect was different. Cannabis gave him energy and instilled a desire to go out and run and play. Later he realized it was the anti-inflammatory properties of cannabis that made him feel better.

Jerry's early commitment to research and promote the healing powers of cannabis was solidified when he met Jack Herer, author of *The Emperor Wears No Clothes: The Authoritative Historical Record of Cannabis and the Conspiracy against Marijuana . . . And How Hemp Can Save the World*,[19] at a Grateful Dead concert. They got on the topic of marijuana and Jack said to him, "I think your generation is going to change the world. Here, read this someday," and handed over a signed copy of his book. Receiving that book marked a defining moment in Jerry's life. (A sample chapter is available at www.JackHerer.com/TheBook/Chapter-Eleven.)

What is interesting is that Jack Herer's book came out in the 1970s, and he proposed a challenge that if anyone could prove any of his theories wrong, he would give them $10,000. That didn't happen, and by the 2000s, he offered $100,000 to prove him wrong. By the time of his death in 2010, no one had taken him up on his offer.

Jerry and his peers at the University of Wyoming formed CAMP, the Coalition Against Marijuana Prohibition, in 1995. CAMP held events to educate people about the healing potential of cannabis.

When Jerry had his first liver transplant in 1997, he was in the hospital for six weeks and at home in recovery for nine weeks. After twelve years of health, the transplanted liver failed. In 2009, he decided to prepare differently for the next liver. He consumed large quantities of cannabis during the weeks prior to his surgery. As soon as he was out of surgery, friends brought him cannabis in the hospital, hidden in food.

Jerry's recovery from his first liver transplant took fifteen weeks. Within a day or two of his second liver transplant, he was able to get out of bed and go outside. He got off the morphine much faster. He got out of the hospital in thirteen days and was back at work within a month.

He opened Medical Marijuana of the Rockies on August 1, 2009. It was the first medical dispensary in Summit County and the mountain regions. (Here's some perspective: Within one year, there were 1,600 to 1,800 dispensaries statewide.)

Jerry's Big Vision

Jerry's main goal was to build a Mayo Clinic version of marijuana dispensaries, a fully functioning hospital for healing with medical marijuana. His plan: to use those profits to fund medical marijuana research and to create something meaningful that would help people for generations to come. I wish I was able to put into words the level of passion with which this man speaks.

For years, it seemed he was on his way. Then, in late 2014, he decided to expand by moving his shop to larger premises. This simple decision led to the downfall of Medical Marijuana of the Rockies, as it incurred the wrath of the nearby Holiday Inn franchise. They blocked the purchase and license, which had already been approved by the town of Frisco. The Holiday Inn brought in the big anti-legalization guns—the Washington-based "Safe Street Alliance."

Together, they filed civil RICO (Racketeer Influenced and Corrupt Organizations) charges against Jerry and everyone involved with the move. Their efforts succeeded. The lawsuit scared away the lenders, tied up the process, and halted construction on the new store. The strong arm of a group outside of Colorado was able to bury Jerry's small business in an insurmountable pile of legal bills, and Medical Marijuana of the Rockies was forced to close its doors.

In an article written by Phil Lindeman on February 19, 2015, the story broke on the front page of the *Summit Daily News*. "Holiday Inn targets Summit County dispensary in first marijuana RICO case" was the banner headline that day. The article begins, "Nearly three months after two heartland states sued Colorado in federal court, a Frisco dispensary is now at the epicenter of the first-ever racketeering lawsuit filed against a marijuana business since the advent of legal weed . . ."[20]

Even with the store closed and in the middle of a federal lawsuit, Jerry had this to say: "This is not over. My convictions are something I expect to hold steady the rest of my life. There is still the goal to build something positive for those in need in this world."

For the latest updates and outcomes, check www.MM-Rockies.com.

Native Roots

Contact Information:
Rhett Jordan
308 South Hunter St.
Aspen, Colorado 81611
www.NativeRoots303.com
970-429-4443

It is impossible for me to drive to Aspen, Colorado, and not think of quotes from my favorite comedy, *Dumb and Dumber*. Believe me, it was all I could do to not sing the Mockingbird song or make "the most annoying sound in the world" while driving there. By the way, I really did go home and watch the movie on the night I interviewed Rhett Jordan in his Aspen dispensary.

It took a little over a month to chase down the busy dispensary owner and creator of the Native Roots brand. No mystery why the man is busy: Native Roots calls itself the "#1 Dispensary in Colorado."

I don't think I could describe the history of this rapidly expanding company better than they do on their own website:

> What began as a medical dispensary on the famous 16th Street Mall in Denver has grown through a partnership with Boulder medical dispensary, The Dandelion, forming the Native Roots Colorado brand. Devoted to quality products and customer experience, Native Roots is synonymous with premium cannabis products including flowers (weed), edibles, and our world-renowned concentrate line—Native Roots Extracts. . . .
>
> With nine stores and counting throughout Colorado, we provide our patients and patrons with quality, accessible cannabis.
>
> We carry a wide selection of marijuana, edibles, BHO extracts including shatter, wax, and live resin, marijuana-infused products, topical alternatives, and an array of accessories. . . .
>
> With plans for continued expansion across the state of Colorado, we look forward to serving the Colorado Cannabis Community for years to come.

The Native Roots Mission

Native Roots Mission Statement

Native Roots Colorado is the premier authority on all things cannabis in Colorado. It is our company's mission to work within each community to provide safe and welcoming facilities that offer a concierge style cannabis shopping experience in an upscale atmosphere. We serve a vast demographic of customers who are local, national, and international. Whether our guests have experience with cannabis, or no experience at all, we place a heavy focus on educating them on all matters relating to cannabis and its responsible consumption while they are with us. We are passionate about our product, our brand, our culture, and our customers.

As Native Roots employees, we are expected to have fun, exemplify a "next level" hospitality experience to all of our customers, support our teammates, take responsibility in each of our roles, and take pride in our work and the Native Roots Brand. Each employee is an integral part of our individual shops success, and the success of our company as a whole.

We are the Native Roots fam and we are a family on a mission.[21]

Rhett Jordan takes his mission statement very seriously. He has been a cannabis advocate for years. He used it successfully himself to help with debilitating back pain from biking and snowboarding injuries.

As a legitimate caregiver (licensed provider/grower of cannabis) [see glossary], he began his journey into cannabis horticulture. The very first plant that he attempted to grow turned out to be extremely successful, and he turned a profit. With the money made from his first plant, Rhett invested in a caregiver facility and began to buy as many books on growing as he could find, which eventually led to his passion for cultivating cannabis.

Possessing all the legal paperwork was essential in keeping Rhett in compliance with all the new laws. However, as a result of a few encounters with law enforcement, he was "invited" to the law enforcement headquarters to describe to officers how much medical marijuana can be grown legally. Sometimes Rhett gave officers who dropped by his grow facility for an unexpected "visit" a tour, so that they could learn firsthand what being completely in compliance with the law actually looks like.

Diesel the Dog Goes to Jail 2009

One of Rhett's favorite stories from the early medical era was when he was pulled over with about fifteen pounds of cannabis as he was heading to a dispensary after a harvest.

On the way from his grow facility to the dispensary, Rhett and one of his growers were pulled over near the city of Parker, cuffed and placed in separate squad cars. Rhett's dog Diesel, who accompanied Rhett everywhere, was taken from Rhett's car to the police pound. Rhett had all the compliance paperwork with him, so he repeatedly requested that the

Parker police contact the South Metro Drug Task Force to confirm that he was transporting the marijuana legally.

Finally, after a couple hours on the phone and reading over Rhett's legal paperwork, they released Rhett and the grower. The grower friend began walking away down the highway after being released in no apparent meaningful direction. He just wanted to get away from the whole ordeal.

The Parker police told Rhett that he was free to go, but "your dog is in jail and your friend ran away." Rhett soon bailed Diesel out of jail, but he never was able to get his traumatized friend back in the car that day.

Strain Knowledge and a Bit of Science

Rhett has travelled the world to meet with growers of cannabis to discuss what he calls "genetics," meaning which strains might combat specific diseases and ailments, and which types of highs are generated by specific strains in recreational use.

Rhett has worked with over a thousand different strains and has grown more than five hundred. He likes to say that he has a personal relationship with each plant and is able to observe characteristics such as node spacing, crystal production, and leaf patterns. At this point in his career, he has been able to hire breeders to begin breeding their own genetics with unique names that create a brand specific to the strain. For example, the first collaboration was with an artist Griz that resulted in a strain called the Griz Kush, which won a Cannabis Cup [see glossary].

The Edible Experience

Under Rhett's guidance, Native Roots has developed a robust program of consumer education about edibles. Rhett feels that not only does education help consumers have a better experience, it brings them back as return customers. If someone consumes too much of an edible and has a bad experience, they are not going to want to come back. That's what's known as a "one and done."

From Native Roots' Edibles Education Pamphlet

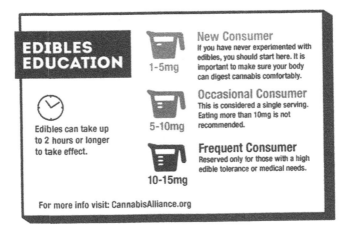

Their warnings are color coded to emulate ski resort terrain categories. Green is beginner, blue is intermediate, and black is for experts.

Below is another example from the Native Roots pamphlet of what a cannabis menu looks like. Flower is the new term replacing the old term of bud and refers to the cannabis that is consumed. *Ex* means *exclusive* and *T* stands for *top shelf.*

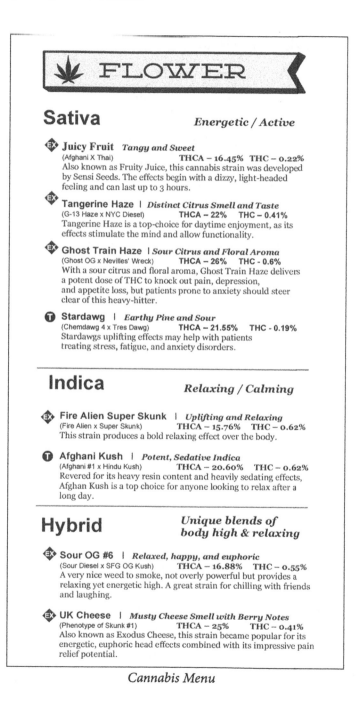

FLOWER

Sativa
Energetic / Active

Juicy Fruit *Tangy and Sweet*
(Afghani X Thai) THCA – 16.45% THC – 0.22%
Also known as Fruity Juice, this cannabis strain was developed
by Sensi Seeds. The effects begin with a dizzy, light-headed
feeling and can last up to 3 hours.

Tangerine Haze | *Distinct Citrus Smell and Taste*
(G-13 Haze x NYC Diesel) THCA – 22% THC – 0.41%
Tangerine Haze is a top-choice for daytime enjoyment, as its
effects stimulate the mind and allow functionality.

Ghost Train Haze | *Sour Citrus and Floral Aroma*
(Ghost OG x Nevilles' Wreck) THCA – 26% THC - 0.6%
With a sour citrus and floral aroma, Ghost Train Haze delivers
a potent dose of THC to knock out pain, depression,
and appetite loss, but patients prone to anxiety should steer
clear of this heavy-hitter.

Stardawg | *Earthy Pine and Sour*
(Chemdawg 4 x Tres Dawg) THCA – 21.55% THC - 0.19%
Stardawgs uplifting effects may help with patients
treating stress, fatigue, and anxiety disorders.

Indica
Relaxing / Calming

Fire Alien Super Skunk | *Uplifting and Relaxing*
(Fire Alien x Super Skunk) THCA – 15.76% THC – 0.62%
This strain produces a bold relaxing effect over the body.

Afghani Kush | *Potent, Sedative Indica*
(Afghani #1 x Hindu Kush) THCA – 20.60% THC – 0.62%
Revered for its heavy resin content and heavily sedating effects,
Afghan Kush is a top choice for anyone looking to relax after a
long day.

Hybrid
Unique blends of body high & relaxing

Sour OG #6 | *Relaxed, happy, and euphoric*
(Sour Diesel x SFG OG Kush) THCA – 16.88% THC – 0.55%
A very nice weed to smoke, not overly powerful but provides a
relaxing yet energetic high. A great strain for chilling with friends
and laughing.

UK Cheese | *Musty Cheese Smell with Berry Notes*
(Phenotype of Skunk #1) THCA – 25% THC – 0.41%
Also known as Exodus Cheese, this strain became popular for its
energetic, euphoric head effects combined with its impressive pain
relief potential.

Cannabis Menu

The Future of Native Roots

"Consistency is key," describes Rhett's business plan. Every-thing, including the design of the shop, the wallpaper, and the quality of the products, is consistent throughout the multiple Native Roots stores in Colorado.

The key to the consistency of the product is that it comes from one centrally located grow house in the Denver area. "With larger grows, it is more important to spend the money on infrastructure to ensure quality. Although we're not trying to be the biggest, we do want to be the best," Rhett says.

CHAPTER 9

The Dealers and the Players

If there are two potheads in the back of a car,
then who is driving?
The cop.

In an effort to gather a complete story from the mountains, I decided to interview anonymous dealers of illegal marijuana.

The first person I talked with was against the legalization of marijuana. Since legalization, the dealer has had to purchase from the recreational stores for their own personal consumption. I don't know whether they're still in the illegal business. I didn't ask, wouldn't tell!

Interview

    Interviewer: Author
    Interviewee: First Anonymous Dealer (Anon)
    Interview Setting: Random grassy knoll

Johnny: Has the legalization of recreational marijuana in Colorado affected your business?

Anon: Yes. There have only been two purchases since January 1, 2014. Prior to that date, it was ten purchases a week.

Johnny: What is your opinion of the quality of marijuana being sold at the recreational dispensaries?

Anon: Lesser grade product and the prices have gone up. Also, the packaging is not recyclable. Plastic pill bottles and plastic security bags are not recyclable.

Johnny: Do you, as a user, feel more comfortable smoking now?

Anon: Feel the same.

Johnny: Are you having a harder time obtaining product to sell?

Anon: Yes, my old sources are selling to the shops.

Johnny: Do you sell edibles?

Anon: No, too labor intensive.

Johnny: Do you agree with the legalization of recreational marijuana?

Anon: No, decriminalization instead of legalization. I feel people are taking advantage of the situation and becoming careless by leaving cannabis around where kids and pets can get to it.

Johnny: Have you lowered or raised your pricing?

Anon: At first it was raised, but then prices came back down because nobody was coming around. Currently prices are less than the stores but higher than before.

I then asked the anonymous dealer how much he was making per year with illegal sales. He answered that he was making about $5000 extra per year and that he never paid for his personal use. So far, this year it is difficult to say, but he hasn't made any money yet. He also has to pay now for his personal use.

Former Trafficker Story

The following story is from a friend who used to live in Summit County, Colorado, before he was arrested for trafficking. Now that he has served his time and now that weed is legal here in Colorado, he elected to share one of his stories. Here it is, as he wrote it.

The Traveling Circus
by H.T. (Ex-illegal dealer and trafficker)

In order to successfully move a couple of thousand pounds of weed from Arizona to Detroit and New York City as frequently as once a month, a number of factors need to be considered. The first thing, undoubtedly, is you don't want to get caught. Especially when it's a game of cat and mouse, and your people are the mice with all the cheese.

It's not as simple as loading a truck with the weed and hitting the open highway. You have to spend money in order to make a lot of it, and you simply can't skimp if you value your freedom. That means putting together two teams of decoy drivers, picking the right inconspicuous couple to drive the actual "package," getting all the right vehicles in place, and hoping the people you work with are people you can trust.

Since the team was essentially comprised of a group of misfits, people who were comfortable living on the edge, I called them my Traveling Circus.

The couple driving the package was usually paid $100 per pound. That's a couple of hundred thousand dollars for driving four ten-hour days, or roughly $2500 an hour, each. Coupled with all the other expenses, each trip would generally cost over a quarter of a million dollars. And it was not unusual to do that as often as once a month. On the other hand, we stood to double our investment once the weed hit New York.

Back when we were getting high-grade commercial product from one of the cartels in Mexico, we could expect to pay anywhere from $500–$1000 multiplied by two thousand pounds (depending on the seasonal availability, quality, and the whims of the supplier). This meant we owed some not-so-very-nice guys a million or two for every load.

For each load of weed, we generally had to move the money back to the cartel in two separate loads. They didn't like to wait very long for it, so as soon as we had a million or so, it needed to hit the road. Oftentimes we were delivering shipments of cash across the country, from the east to the southwest, every few weeks. We couldn't simply wire the money, so that presented yet another challenge: getting cash from New York City and Detroit to Arizona without losing it to law enforcement that was constantly on the lookout for cash couriers. In states like Kansas, they fund their departments with the money they confiscate in "traffic" stops. If you can't prove where you got it, they get to keep it. Consequently, moving quantities of cash and product through these states required meticulous planning and execution of many moving parts. On top of that, money is bulky, heavy, and generally an inconvenient pain in the ass. Sounds absolutely ridiculous, but it's never given to you in hundred dollar bills, so a million dollars in mostly twenties is well over a hundred pounds. You don't leave it in the car or hand it off to the bellman (who would undoubtedly wonder why your luggage is so damn heavy). Instead, you're lugging it into hotels along the way and babysitting it rather than going out to a nice dinner. You're always on edge, always looking over your shoulder, always aware that the proverbial shoe could drop at any time during the trip.

If I were traveling across the country with more than a million dollars, I would have a decoy car and driver(s) in a rented Lincoln with New York plates. This was especially attractive to lawmen in some of the hardest states: Kansas, Nebraska, Arizona, New Mexico, and Utah. We could count on the Lincolns being pulled over in these places. Since they all bordered or were near Colorado, I often drove the cash in my Jeep sporting Colorado plates. Every few cars traveling in those states had similar plates, and Jeeps were as common as Subarus in the state.

My Jeep fit right in. This allowed us to move more comfortably through these states with the cash. When we did our weed runs, the aim was to remain as inconspicuous as possible. Hence, on those runs, the "package" (usually weighing in at a hefty two thousand pounds) was sure to travel in a trailer attached to an SUV, both with Colorado plates.

The weed runs would require the circus to hit the road. This would involve the two Lincolns, my Jeep as the "mission control," and the package in a trailer being pulled by a new

Suburban or Excursion (which broke down twice). For this, the decoys would be rented Lincolns with Arizona plates. Not inconspicuous at all. More often than not, the moment a decoy crossed into any of the bordering states, it would be pulled over within a matter of minutes. That's why we'd have two Lincolns, so we wouldn't be slowed down too much when one was on the side of the road getting searched. An added bonus was that if a Lincoln was pulled over, it gave us time for a lunch break while we waited for them to catch up to us. The targeted decoy would never do anything to actually justify a traffic stop, but simply driving a rented Lincoln with Arizona plates was usually sufficient cause for the troopers. More often than not, to increase our odds, we'd pair a white guy with a black girl, or vice versa, to catch their possibly racist eye. Finally, we would only drive during daylight hours, so the troopers would be more enticed by what we had put in front of them. Once pulled over, the decoys would always be asked to consent to a search of the vehicle. Refusing only took longer, since the troopers would then call out a canine unit. This would inevitably result in the dog "reacting," giving the officers "grounds for a search." Usually they'd ask the drivers to wait in the back of the cruiser while they conducted their search. All of this "switch and bait" kept the troopers busy, allowing the rest of the circus to travel unnoticed. One particularly funny incident happened when we were driving a "package" to New York. Just as we crossed into Nebraska, my lead decoy got pulled over. On this particular instance, my friend Mr. M wanted to have a little fun with the state patrol. Sitting in the back seat of the cruiser, knowing that they were being recorded, Mr. M said to his companion, "Look at the way that trooper's leaning in right behind the other one. You know they fuck! That one's the bottom, and the guy that looks like he's grinding on him, he's the top. I'd sure like to see them going at it." Once the search concluded, they asked my team to wait back in their rented vehicle while they listened to the recording, hoping to find something incriminating. Instead, they got to hear Mr. M spewing a rather graphic description of their homosexual activities. One red-faced officer came back to Mr. M's window, yelling while pointing his finger in his face, "Get the fuck out of my state and don't let me catch you here again!" And, of course, by this time, the product was dozens of miles down the road.

I was retelling that story to a group of friends over lunch one day in Breckenridge. I was surprised that Mr. M barely remembered it. It was probably because of all the run-ins and near misses he had over the course of our hundreds of thousands of miles across this great land of ours.

And no, we never got caught. We were just told on.

Interview

Interviewer: Author
Interviewee: Anonymous Dealer (Anon)
Setting: Somewhere in Frisco

Johnny: Where were you based out of?
Anon: I was living and growing marijuana in Leadville, Colorado. I was selling all sizes and quantities and receiving larger shipments of pounds from California.

Johnny: What would you say you earned in your days of dealing?

Anon: Over the course of four years, I probably made around $200 thousand before I retired.

Johnny: Did you ever get caught or have any close calls?

Anon: Never got caught but I got pulled over one time with sixty pounds in the trunk and wasn't searched, so I got away with that one. There were times when I got paid to just drive the marijuana in from other states. The very last time I was involved in trafficking was when I had to fly to California with cash and had to have another person fly with me because it was too heavy.

Johnny: Any funny stories that you remember?

Anon: Yes. One time I had to go and pick up some friends who got stranded in the desert because their plane broke down and wasn't able to continue to fly. I had to go and pick up two people, three dogs, and three large, dry bags full of weed in some tiny town of three hundred people at one little emergency landing airstrip.

Johnny: You've been retired for over ten years now and have invested in other businesses. Would you ever go back into selling pot illegally again?

Anon: No, that whole business model is gone. It doesn't exist anymore. I will say it was fun while it lasted. But now that recreational marijuana is legal in Colorado, it's safer to enter into the industry through the legal ways. There's still money to be made.

CHAPTER 10

Weedia: Weed in the Media

In this chapter you will find everything from little tidbits of information to events visited and everything in between. Enjoy.

Cannabis Capital Summit
Hosted by Rockies Venture Club

Investors from around the globe came to Denver, Colorado, on May 29, 2014, for the first ever Cannabis Capital Summit. I could not believe all the ancillary businesses that were springing up left and right from this new industry. The hard part is making sure all the new laws, rules, and regulations are followed, even as they are changing almost weekly. The other large hurdle is the banking issue. Since banks are backed by the Federal Reserve, they cannot touch any cash from many of the businesses in this industry. Many are forced to operate the same way dispensaries do as cash only.

The 2014 Summit was full of expo booths on two levels ranging from hemp, raising capital, grow lights, greenhouses, food and beverages, healthcare, marketing, advertising, taking a company public, packaging, and software to name a few. Speakers and panel discussions were held on the lower level as well as pitches from companies to potential investors. The panel discussions were thorough and full of valuable information dealing with banking, investing, the future of legalization, and ancillary businesses. Networking breaks were scheduled throughout the day and were the busiest part of the conference. I met Ricardo Baca from The Cannabist, the "Rolling Papers" documentary crew, and a reality show crew from Stoner, Colorado, that was working on a pilot about one entrepreneur's plan to rebuild the town of Stoner, Colorado, as the global center for all things cannabis.

The Cannabist

I had the pleasure of chatting with Ricardo Baca, the marijuana editor of The Denver Post's The Cannabist, at the Cannabis Capital Summit, and interviewing him again a few months later at the offices of The Denver Post. The Cannabist identifies itself as a "place of ideas, people, art, food and news" about "the culture of cannabis."[22] It's affiliated with The Denver Post. The site itself is a cannabis-related success story, from its origin as a relatively small experimental blog, to its current status as a comprehensive resource site for newsworthy stories about the marijuana not just in Colorado, but worldwide, with a writing staff that includes guest columnist Whoopi Goldberg. I highly recommend this site for a wealth of information and great writing on this topic. This site and the Facebook page www.Facebook.com/Cannabist both earn my "Author's Choice" award.

We met at *The Denver Post* building in downtown Denver and talked on the rooftop of the building. To me, Ricardo is *The Cannabist*. He was the entertainment and music critic for *The Denver Post* before becoming its marijuana editor. When I ask him about his reputation as a journalist now that he writes about marijuana, Baca said that there has been no damage to his reputation. In fact, there has been an increase in readership.

The Cannabist displays most of its content online. There is definitely no shortage of stories. Baca recalls doing a piece on THC-infused massage oils and pain lotions for a massage business in the Denver area, and they reported back that on the day of the article, they received over thirty calls in less than twenty-four hours.

One cool aspect that I learned from Baca was that *The Cannabist* has a content-sharing agreement with *High Times Magazine*. Baca writes anywhere from zero to six articles per day. After receiving the new job title, Baca was invited on *The View* and became the pun for some witty marijuana jokes on late night talk shows, including *The O'Reilly Factor*. After the first three months of that level of excitement, it began to subside a bit.

"Now that we are past the six-month mark, the excitement levels have turned into business as usual."

—Ricardo Baca

The Director of the Documentary *Rolling Papers*

Mitch Dickman is an award-winning producer and director in both film and theatre. He is the founder and director of Denver-based Listen Productions, a full-service media production company. His credits include the feature films *Hanna Ranch* and *A Test of Wills*, the Honduran travel show *Off the Radar*, the short film *Mortar* (2006 Starz Denver Film Festival Official Selection), and the stage production and feature documentary film DNC Mediamockracy.[23]

Interview

> **Interviewer:** Author
> **Interviewee:** Mitch Dickman, director of *Rolling Papers*
> **Setting**: I interviewed Mitch while he was still working on the film.

Johnny: Who is Mitch Dickman? What is your background?

Mitch: I came from a little town in Missouri to live in Colorado and enjoy Copper Mountain Ski Resort. I went to CU Boulder and studied film, TV, and theater. At first I wasn't into films and filming. That passion happened a couple of years after I started college. I've done some documentaries, narrative films, and some live theater.

Johnny: What inspired you to film a documentary about the marijuana industry in Colorado?

Mitch: It's a funny thing. I actually wasn't inspired. I remember being on a set for a piece on Evel Knievel and learned of a film about the medical marijuana industry that was started and then lost steam. It was one of the hottest topics in Colorado, and we had a chance to pick up and do the documentary as told through the characters in the film. The characters are the staff members and freelancers of *The Cannabist* and *The Denver Post*. I have no stance either way when it comes to recreational marijuana, which makes for a better story. I met up with Ricardo Baca on January 1, and we decided to create the documentary from a sort of "fly on the wall" type style of reporting. It helps to not be too embedded on either side of an issue. Otherwise it's easy to have a bit of bias.

Johnny: What is the goal of the film?

Mitch: To tell a never-seen-before story through characters at *The Denver Post* and have fun with it. Hopefully we will sell it to a distributor and have it released sometime next year.

Johnny: What kind of responses are you receiving so far?
Mitch: Most of the interest in the documentary is coming from out of state. We are in a fishbowl for the world to look at right now, and of course, there is the stigma of marijuana. The media generally are the ones giggling every time the subject is brought up.

Johnny: What have been the biggest hurdles so far?

Mitch: Financing was tricky. There are a lot of marijuana businesses happening right now in all areas of commerce, so there is a lot of competition. The other hurdle was how to tell the story.

Johnny: What has been the funniest story so far?

Mitch: The 420 weekend was intense. There was the Cannabis Cup and the celebration over at Denver's Civic Center Park and we had two journalists that don't even smoke marijuana and were thrown right into the mix.

Johnny: I understand there has been some travel associated with the film. What was that like?

Mitch: We did travel to Uruguay as part of following Ricardo Baca and his visit there. Uruguay just recently passed the legalization of marijuana as well. A big difference between Colorado and Uruguay is that in Uruguay marijuana is legal on the federal level whereas in Colorado it is legal throughout the state but still against federal law. Also in the United States, the majority of the people support the legalization of marijuana and the government opposes it. In Uruguay, the government supports it, but the majority of people do not. Uruguay is a little behind when it comes to writing the rules and regulations regarding the legalization.

Johnny: Can we expect to see anyone famous in the documentary?

Mitch: Not really, although Whoopi Goldberg is a guest columnist for *The Cannabist*. Ricardo Baca was on *The View* as the new marijuana editor, and Whoopi showed some interest in the hot new topic.

Johnny: You mentioned in an interview that it was a bold decision for *The Denver Post* to hire a marijuana editor. They hired Ricardo Baca. How has that been going?

Mitch: It's been a great success, and yes, it was a bold decision. It is an interesting and unique opportunity and so far is going well. Baca is doing a great job on focusing on the cultural side of the industry.

Interview with Frank McDonald, Owner of Stoner, Colorado

Entrepreneur Frank McDonald hopes to resurrect and rebuild a whole town in Colorado, giving it a cannabis theme. He believes this will create hundreds of new jobs, be profitable, be philanthropic, and become a must-visit destination for marijuana enthusiasts. Complete with a music venue, lodging, greenhouses, and research center, he sees it as a potential mecca of the cannabis world.

Stoner is located just south of Telluride in the southwest part of the state. It's situated in a beautiful valley nestled among the majestic mountain peaks and Dolores River. The only resident is a gal named Mary Jane, according to McDonald.

McDonald bought the whole town, in April 2011, while lying in a hospital bed. Ironically, he was there because of renal cell carcinoma and having had half of his kidney removed. But after the removal, tumors were still forming. He began taking cannabis oils in high concentrations, and upon his return visit to the doctors, the tumors were gone. He gives credit to medical marijuana for helping him recover and battle new cancer cells.

I had the great pleasure of meeting Frank McDonald at the 2014 Cannabis Capital Summit in Denver. A film crew was following him around as they documented the highlights of attempting to create a marijuana town. I was impressed by the pilot of this reality show in the making by producer Kat King. I first met Kat outside the event; in fact, she was the one who told me about Frank. She said I must meet this charismatic character named Frank McDonald, and she explained to me what he was planning.

I first saw McDonald standing outside the event, wearing a big cowboy hat and tattoo sleeves on both arms. He was surrounded by camera crews. Kat filled him in on what I was up to with the book, and we hit it off right away. He plans to have Tommy Chong (of Cheech and Chong) play the chief of police in the film, and he has expressed some interest. I hope this happens.

I could tell Frank was focused and driven by his belief in the medical healing properties of cannabis. He was so polite and respectful when we spoke, and he agreed to do a conference call interview, which we accomplished almost half a year later. He described to me his vision and plans for his big goal and suggested I reprint his vision as written in the pitch for the documentary. Here is Frank's story according to Frank . . . as of late 2015 none of these dates had been met, but Frank insists he's still committed.

According to Frank

Frank had purchased the property with a goal of someday developing it as a place for growing legal medical marijuana and providing it to cancer patients and children with seizures. A partnership was formed with Daren Carei and Synergy Wise Builders, with Martin Tindell of Phoenix Pharms Capital Corporation on board as consultants.

Stoner Colorado Inc. would become the holding company for the town and surrounding assets. The goal would be to build sixteen acres of greenhouses for the legal production of cannabis, a treatment center, and a production center, and creating up to three hundred new jobs in Stoner.

Future plans include incorporation of the town and the assessment of excise duty on all cannabis products grown or produced within the town limits, whereby the collected revenue would be used to fund a treatment center and to provide access to families without the financial means to gain access to medical services.

Cannabis production in Stoner will be focused on two separate market segments for the safe and legal access to cannabis.

1. Medical products. Proprietary extracted cannabinoids from the cannabis plant infused into medical delivery systems.

2. Adult use recreational marijuana. High-quality flower and concentrates.

The plan is to sell all products through licensed dispensaries throughout the state of Colorado, including a planned dispensary for the town.

McDonald and Royal Interactive Studios are currently working on a new docuseries about the historical rebirth of the town of Stoner.

Next time you ask, "Where's your weed grown?" The answer will be, "Stoner, Colorado. Where else?"

From my conference call with Frank and Martin Tindell, I learned of their passion to help others. If they should be successful, they plan to give back to the community.

I'm excited to see how their plans to build an "old school" Wild West Main Street complete with apothecary and dispensary turn out. It sounds like a great center for pot tourism.

Cannabis Film

The first year of legalization spawned (at least) a documentary, a reality show, and even a pot movie *Boulder Buddz*, which is a pot comedy by Colorado filmmaker David W. Gray. The story, set in 2010, is about a burned-out, black-market pot dealer struggling with the transition to medical marijuana.

Gray cut his teeth making ski movies. (He has also worked in the medical cannabis industry.) He founded Boulder Independent Productions, with producer Philippa Burgess, to produce his first theatrical feature film. According to Philippa, together they've garnered support and raised money from the local community to cover production, marketing, and distribution costs. To learn more about this film, scheduled for release in late 2016, visit www.BoulderBuddz.com. The movie is about weed, and it wouldn't have been possible to make without the support from those in the cannabis industry. Phillipa told me they have also found everyone they've worked with at the Screen Actors Guild, in the Colorado film community, and in the Boulder government offices to be incredibly helpful.

Local Newspapers

Ads

I loved opening my local Summit County newspapers during the first year of legalization. The ads struck me as so funny, so unlikely, so local. I thought you might enjoy seeing some of them.

Speaking of newspapers, here's a revealing tidbit: the *Summit Daily News* online site includes the following categories under its "news" tab: Crime, Obituaries, Regional, Sports & Outdoors, Announcements, and Marijuana. There is even a new category in the print classified section for marijuana dispensaries—right between land and garden supplies and medical supplies.

Local Articles

I see this book, in part, as a sort of time capsule representation of the zaniness and obsession that captivated Colorado during the first year of marijuana legalization. Nothing tells the story better, I think, than some of the front-page small-town newspaper headlines of the time.

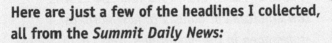

Here are just a few of the headlines I collected, all from the *Summit Daily News:*

- *"Pot bolsters Colorado tourism: Recent study suggests traveler interest in the state has increased by 20% since recreational marijuana first hit the market"* (Aug 27, 2014)

- *"Breckenridge PD launches 'Eat Responsibly' campaign for marijuana edibles"* (May 19, 2014)

- *"Will traffic deaths rise as states legalize pot?"* (Sept 2, 2014)

- *"Colorado Symphony Orchestra links up with pot industry"* (April 30, 2014)

- *"Hash oil explosions up with legalized pot"* (May 7, 2014)

- *"Lawmakers approve long-shot plan for pot banking"* (May 9, 2014)

- *"Lawmakers weigh new pot rules: Legislation aims to adjust possession limits on concentrates, fund study on health effects"* (May 6, 2014)

- *"In Colorado, a pot holiday tries to go mainstream"* (April 21, 2014)

- *"Recreational pot is here, now what? Communities adjust to new laws while trying to keep weed away from children"* (March 10, 2014)

- *"Police officers watch weed industry evolve: Law enforcement adjusts to new norm as stores open in the mountains"* (March 11, 2014)

- *"Legal Pot in Colo. hasn't stopped black market"* (April 5, 2014)

- *"Student death related to pot cookie"* (April 4, 2014)

- *"Reefer revenue tops $2 million: Breck retail pot banks $38K from local tax in first month of legalization"* (March 12, 2014)

- *"January retail pot taxes yield millions in revenue for Colo."* (March 12, 2014)

- *"Polis introduces pot impairment guidelines and immigration bill"* (March 10, 2014) (Notice how pot is mentioned first in this headline over the immigration issue.)

- *"New Rules for marijuana businesses: Standards released by the state Marijuana Enforcement Division include regulations on safety, health training, testing requirements and edibles"* (Sept 29, 2014)

- *"Summit County Sheriff's marijuana FAQ hits the streets"* (March 24, 2014)

- *"Marijuana bud showing up in craft beers"* (March 13, 2014) (This will be fun for my bartending LOL.)

- *"Marijuana explained: What are concentrates and how are they used?"* (March 28, 2014)

- *"Marijuana vessels: joints, pipes, bongs, bats and other ways to smoke"* (March 28, 2014)

Amnesty Drop Boxes in Airports

There are now amnesty drop-off boxes located in airports where people can drop off any marijuana they have on them before boarding a flight. It is illegal to possess marijuana in the airport but an even bigger crime to take it out of state. So for those who may have "somehow" forgotten to get rid of their weed prior to entering the airport, they can now drop it in the amnesty box before boarding a plane. Officials are seeing quite a bit of prescription meds as well as vape pens, pipes, hash, and marijuana.

Get Baked with Seth Rogen and Watch His Movie

On December 1, 2014, I saw an open public invitation sent by Canadian actor Seth Rogen to come and watch the screening of *The Interview*, in which he stars with James Franco. The actor tweeted that he would "get baked" with the entire audience in Denver, Colorado, before watching the action comedy together.[24]

Since Colorado had recently legalized recreational marijuana, Rogen wanted to bring the audience's moviegoing experience to the next level. How funny is that! I sent my e-mail in to RSVP for this event and received this auto-reply: "Thank you for your interest in seeing THE INTERVIEW. Unfortunately the screening is now full." Darn, I wonder how close I was to getting in.

Only a few hours after the e-mail I learned that the event had been changed, and tequila would be served instead of cannabis. Seth poured tequila straight from the bottle into the mouths of many moviegoers.

Given the fact that the movie instigated a North Korean hacking scandal that rocked Sony execs, cost the company millions of dollars, and included more than a few death threats, I kind of think some calming cannabis would have been a much better choice for the screening than tequila.

CHAPTER 11

Cannabis Controversies

"Today is 4/20. This is like national pot day. And people
celebrate all over the world. Although, I must say,
the Senate did not celebrate this by smoking joints,
for two reasons. One, it would be against protocol.
And two, it would mean passing something."
—Bill Maher, *Real Time with Bill Maher*

Edibles

When pot was first legalized in Colorado, many of us joked about edibles after hearing stories of people who consumed way too much cannabis, without realizing it, and did silly things. As time went on, though, we all realized that pot accidentally over-consumed after being baked into common foods like cookies and gummy bears was often not a laughing matter.

Over-consumption of edibles may be the biggest controversy that Colorado faced in the first six months of legalization. Edibles were popular at the start of legalization. No one then really knew what to expect when it came to the amount of edibles people would be eating, and the packaging wasn't strict or consistent. Top all that off with the American addiction to sugar, and it was common to see people eat a whole pot-infused chocolate bar when the label recommended dividing the bar into ten separate doses.

We soon began to hear the stories of people consuming edibles, not feeling anything, eating more, and ending up in the hospital. There can be devastating outcomes with the use of edibles—2014 saw three deaths related to over-consumption.

Be sure to check out the excellent and revealing *New York Times* article written by Maureen Dowd called, "Don't Harsh Our Mellow, Dude."[25] In the article, she describes her experience in coming to Colorado and consuming edible cannabis in the spirit of investigative journalism.

Colorado learned very quickly to aggressively control edibles. Within a few months of legalization, the state had moved to revise the packaging, labeling, and recommended serving size of edibles. There was also a big push to educate people about responsible consumption. Leading the way on this front were the dispensaries and the budtenders.

Budtenders now warn people to only consume the recommended portion size. I say read those labels and listen to the budtenders. Keep all cannabis-infused food far, far away from children and pets.

Packaging Issue Lessons Learned

The issues with packaging took some figuring out. The packaging needs to be childproof for products that don't have a childproof seal. So now there are thick plastic packages with locking zippers. Some shops have implemented a policy that if you return five of these bags back to the dispensary, you will receive a free joint. The packaging laws keep changing. For the most current laws visit www.Colorado.gov/Revenue.

A Johnny Bartender Observation

The "great big edibles debacle" that happened in the first six months of legalization in Colorado probably will never happen again in other states. I heard way too many stories from behind the bar about how people consumed too much and became "couch locked." Hopefully other states will learn from this and regulate the packaging, labeling, and dosages from the very beginning.

Lava Lamp Holding Room

On the Lighter Side of the Edibles Situation

I have a friend in the Denver area who is a nurse at one of the local hospitals. She told me that her hospital has seen so many patients who have over-consumed that the staff has developed an inside joke. "There should be," say the staff, "a waiting or holding room with lava lamps, velvet posters, and music from the 1960s and 1970s where patients can ride out their high after eating too many edibles." (I should say the people who went to the ER did the right thing—consuming too much cannabis can lead to a high that is frightening, even though in most cases the problem resolves in a few hours. The correct course of action is to go to the ER.)

A Johnny Bartender Observation

"I Won't Come Back!"

A bar customer told me a story I found funny. A wealthy out-of-state man, who had been skiing in Colorado for years, posted, all over social media, that, thanks to the legalization of cannabis, he would never come back and that Colorado would suffer without his money or that of his friends and family. We found that pretty funny in the bar. What did he think had been going on in the high country before now? At least now it's out in the open, and it is definitely illegal to smoke pot at any ski resort.

Illustration by Ryan Spencer

Interview with Summit County Sheriff

This book would not be complete without the input of our local law enforcement. I interviewed Summit County Sheriff John Minor, about halfway through legalization's first year, on August 11, 2014. He welcomed me professionally and treated me, as well as the topic of the legalization of marijuana in Colorado, with great respect. Although I have been impressed with the character and integrity of the unique cannabis businesses, I am equally if not more impressed with our Sheriff John Minor. The depth of his knowledge and the range of his experiences were above and beyond what I had expected. I learned a lot from our meeting.

Our meeting started off with Sheriff Minor showing me some photos of incidents that have happened here in Summit County. Normally, as a bartender, I get to see people having a good time when they are out and about. When that good time goes bad, that's when the sheriff's office gets called.

The first photo showed a hash oil explosion. The process of using butane to cook the hash to get the oil can be dangerous and needs to be in a licensed controlled environment. Butane is extremely flammable and can be devastating in a multi-unit condo complex (See page 167).

He then showed me photos of dangerous electrical wiring in some home growing operations and also photos of some of the chemicals and insecticides used in a home growing operation. And he showed me pictures of boxes wrapped in Christmas paper disguised as holiday gifts that were really packages of weed to be shipped by the postal service.

For the most part, the sheriff said that he didn't really like the idea of legalizing marijuana, but he supported it. The law enforcement's stance is one of safety and responsibility first. I have seen the same willingness to follow laws and rules in the dispensary owners, who don't want to ruin a good thing.

Interview

Interviewer: Author
Interviewee: John Minor, Summit County Sheriff
Setting: Summit County, CO

Johnny: What has been the biggest challenge so far with the legalization of recreational marijuana?

Sheriff Minor: The law trying to catch up with the booming industry. If there isn't a definitive way to regulate the edibles, there's a possibility that the laws could reverse course and make them illegal. There's also an issue with the e-cigarettes or electronic cigarette. People are saying that all they are doing is smoking an e-cigarette when they are really smoking hash oils or other concentrates.

Johnny: What has been the worst consistent problem?

Sheriff Minor: Overdosing on edibles. We are seeing about one every two weeks. Also there's flamboyant use of marijuana where some think it is okay to flaunt the fact in public. They will be arrested.

Johnny: Are there any pros to such an experiment?

Sheriff Minor: We are not wasting as much time on arresting for just marijuana under an ounce. However, even though carrying under an ounce is legal under Amendment 64, it is a felony offense to bring any marijuana into the justice center.

So if we arrest someone, and we ask if they are carrying marijuana on them and they do not disclose this, it is now a felony offense.

Johnny: So if someone is arrested for any reason, they need to disclose that they are carrying marijuana even though they might be within the legal limits of the law.

Sheriff Minor: That's correct. This is also new for the training of officers. They now ask suspects if they are carrying marijuana when arresting.

Johnny: Has there been an increase in arrests?

Sheriff Minor: About 80 percent of all arrests include alcohol or drugs or both. Alcohol is easier to prove by way of Breathalyzer so that gets more focus.

Johnny: Are there more or less incidents regarding just alcohol?

Sheriff Minor: Same.

Johnny: As far as edibles go and the discovery of the potency and issues surrounding them, do you think that the state of Colorado is handling this well?

Sheriff Minor: There's about a year or two more to go before they have it all dialed in. We are dealing with constant new training in this area. I don't think it is too far off until there are mobile units with testing devices to test the amount of THC in the blood. There will be new equipment and new training available, which creates a whole new business model on the law enforcement side, as well as those in the industry itself.

Johnny: Are the dispensary owners helpful? And how are they handling all of this?

Sheriff Minor: Yes, they are helpful. I have even given a talk/community meeting with them, called "The Good, the Bad, and the Ugly," regarding the new industry. We do work well together because they are entrepreneurs and smart. They are trying to abide by the laws. The reputable ones are anyway.

Johnny: Are there more problems with alcohol or pot?

Sheriff Minor: It is too hard to tell if someone is just drunk or drunk and stoned.

Johnny: How do you think this experiment will play out?

Sheriff Minor: I think most of the country will go toward limited legalization, but it may take decades. We have a unique system here in Colorado where the citizens can petition to have a measure put on a ballot. If Colorado fails in this attempt, then the whole experiment will fail. If they succeed, then other states will follow suit. They have until about 2016 to get it all sorted out because that's when there will be a change in the White House and Cabinet. It must be managed well and regulated.

Johnny: Are you surprised by the preliminary state revenue figures?

Sheriff Minor: No, but I feel the allocation of the revenue should have gone to research first, then law enforcement training, then the schools.

Johnny: What could be done to make things more efficient?

Sheriff Minor: I'm not 100 percent sure on that one, but the law needs to catch up and stay flexible. Possibly increase penalties for violations in public.

Alas, Poor Smoke Shack, They Knew You Too Well

One ironic outcome of cannabis legalization was the destruction of the secret shack hidden away on the Vail ski slopes known as "Lee's." Pot smokers in the know had skied off the beaten path and into the hand-built shack to smoke pot on the slopes for years. One such local, Chris Hoover, contended in a *Summit County News* editorial that such shacks can commonly be found, if you know where to look, on many runs at many ski resorts. Hoover said in his editorial that his beloved "Lee's" was taken down by powers-that-be, when pot became legal, in order to make a political statement against the legalization of pot. I take no side in this controversy, other than to say I have a feeling those needing to smoke on the slopes will always find a way—and will always risk arrest and accident by doing so.

Large Increase of Postal Violations

People are mailing marijuana, edibles, wax, and oils out of state. It is illegal to mail marijuana, either in state or out of state, but that hasn't stopped folks from trying.

Nebraska and Oklahoma Sue Colorado

In December 2014, two neighboring states, Nebraska and Oklahoma, sued Colorado in the Supreme Court for legalizing marijuana. The two states claimed that since marijuana was illegal federally, the Colorado legalization put stress on their law enforcement at the borders and created a dangerous situation.

Vape Pen Issue

There have been several issues with customers using vape pens in the bars where I work, and, I'm sure, elsewhere. We are not going to grab the pen and check to see whether tobacco or marijuana is inside the pen, and anyway customers always say that it is tobacco when questioned. The problem is that the smokers feel that because there is no smoke, they should be allowed to hit it wherever they want. Even though it isn't smoke, the perception from other paying guests is that *there is someone smoking in the restaurant.* There will be ordinances passed very soon that will treat vape pens the same as cigarettes and will include the rule about being twenty feet outdoors from any establishment. I bet this will cause a lot of debates.

Kicked Out of Main Street in Breckenridge

One of the biggest controversies to hit the town of Breckenridge was the removal of an existing dispensary from Main Street by way of a special vote. A nonbinding vote influenced the town council to ban retail dispensaries from Main Street. As a result, The Breckenridge Cannabis Club had to pack up and leave Main Street in early February 2015. This story was featured in a CNN original series called, "High Profits."

CHAPTER 12

Weed vs. Alcohol

If you substitute marijuana for tobacco and alcohol,
you'll add eight to twenty-four years to your life.
—Jack Herer, marijuana activist and author[26]

Many people die from alcohol use. Very few die from marijuana use.

"The U.S. Centers for Disease Control and Prevention (CDC) reports that more than 37,000 annual U.S. deaths, including more than 1,400 in Colorado, are attributed to alcohol use alone (i.e. this figure does not include accidental deaths). On the other hand, the CDC does not even have a category for deaths caused by the use of marijuana as of this writing."[27] See Appendix for more statistics and other objective sources. Also go to Recovery First's web page for an easy to read chart on the comparison between the two substances.[28]

Where do I begin on this one? I have to write what I see. It is possible to study the living hell out of this subject and I've tried. But I'm wary of studies and surveys. I wonder who or what corporation pays for certain studies. I get the feeling that a company can get whatever result they are looking for by structuring a study a certain way.

As a server of alcohol, I have witnessed countless and endless altercations, issues, fights, arguments, breakups, makeups, hookups, depression, laughter, tears, loss of inhibitions, arrests, deaths, and overall borderline behavior. I could even go so far as to use the word atrocities. Some events are so bad that I am unable to recount them in this book. Most of my experiences are good when I bartend at a restaurant. But when I bartended at clubs or pub-style places the majority of the people behaved themselves appropriately and a few acted in a way that I would consider offensive, hostile, or illegal.

I hope my next statement doesn't generate further controversy. But I do know what certain types of people prefer when they are out at a bar when it comes to consuming booze or smoking the weed. This is an extremely small town. In other words, I know who is using what.

In people who smoke weed without consuming alcohol, I observe laughter, hunger, relaxation, and an occasional lack of motivation. I don't see the violence or hostility I see in drinkers. So in my opinion—and this is only my opinion—I think that marijuana is less detrimental than alcohol when it comes to behavior.

Fun Flashbacks from the Author

My best example? My own life. Who am I anyway to talk about marijuana and alcohol without stories of my own? Here are some stories from my own experiences with cannabis and with alcohol. My hopes are that the reader can see what each drug has the potential of doing and maybe be entertained by the silliness of the stories. I have omitted or changed the names of all parties involved to protect their identities, except my brother. I only have one brother, and I can't pass him off as a Mike, Joe, or Julio.

Any trouble I got into in my twenties and thirties almost always involved alcohol. I think I have always been ten years behind my actual age when it comes to maturity (just ask my girlfriend), so I made many poor decisions. The worst of these decisions were alcohol induced. Don't worry, I have learned from my mistakes—I hope!

I remember going on ski trips where marijuana was present. (This is also a time when I tried but couldn't seem to inhale.) All we did for a week was cook big meals, watch movies, and play games. We never made it skiing. I remember a lot of laughter as well.

Parental Forgiveness Waiver

Before I tell these stories, I must include here the Parental Forgiveness Waiver for Mom and Dad.

Parental Forgiveness Waiver:
I am hereby released from scowls, scorns, guilt trips, and any other method of parental backlash. Once these stories pass the five-year mark, or one has already "gotten away with it," we shall be forever forgiven.

The Fort Knocka No More Story

During a ski trip to the Pocono Mountains in Pennsylvania, our posse consisted of a large group of buddies in our late teens and early twenties, our parents, and our siblings. We all stayed together in a big ski house away from the resort. My buddies and I knew that our parents were avid wildlife watchers, so we adopted this hobby as well. It was a great excuse to say that we saw deer in the backyard and run outside to smoke pot.

One time, we had all ran outside after watching *Last of the Mohicans*, which had made us run faster, to find these elusive deer. Somehow, we all had found time to smoke, and we had begun to wander deeper into the woods. In between hearty spells of laughter, we found a tree fort. Immediately we began to suggest nicknames for this giant tree fortress made of one sheet of crooked and broken plywood and about three rotting two-by-fours. "Let's call it Fort of the Mohicans!" "Let's call it Fort Nagasaki!" "Let's call it Fort Knocka Down!" The last suggestion for a nickname meant that we had it in our minds to knock it down, which a swift breeze could have done.

I scampered up the tree and perched myself on the uneven plywood. Behind me was my best friend, Carlitos we'll call him. The rest of the crew was down on the ground chanting and cheering and laughing their asses off. We were about eight feet up on this platform and began to wobble like crazy. I spotted a branch above my head and began to formulate a plan in my enlightened state of mind. I figured to myself that if I grabbed hold of the branch above my head and stamped hard on the platform simultaneously, I could break free the plywood and send Carlitos to the ground while I watched safely hanging from my savior of a branch. (Don't worry. The ground below was as soft as a giant sponge due to years of decomposing and fresh leaves.)

Here it goes. I grabbed the branch, jumped on the platform, the platform broke, there went Carlitos tumbling to the ground, my plan was working. Then my branch had broken, and here I had come falling with the rest of the rotting two-by-fours, a few more branches, and a tree load of leaves. After about two seconds, we were all on the ground. It had taken us about a half hour to catch our breaths from the uproarious laughter that probably had echoed right back to the chaperones, who had been safely ensconced inside the house and nowhere near Fort Knocka No More. For years after, simply mentioning the name of our fallen fort brought smiles and laughter to those who were there and those who heard the story of us legends in the woods.

The Boat Antenna Story

A bong is a term used for a type of smoking device that passes the smoke through water and then fills a chamber. The water acts as a type of filter. Once the chamber is full of smoke, an opening is created, usually by taking your thumb off of a pre-made hole. This allows air to go in so that the smoker can inhale and pull the smoke out of the chamber. Bongs come in all shapes, sizes, and art forms.

Back in my college days, I somehow came into possession of a five-foot red bong, also known to those in our circle as a five-footer or "Sleepy." We called it "Sleepy" because after a few hits from this behemoth, you became very comfortable, especially on a couch.

If I recall correctly, which many times I don't, I became Sleepy's guardian because nobody else wanted to take home a five-foot bong after graduation. It would be rather difficult to explain to one's parents that we only used the bong on weekends when we were finished studying. Sleepy came in a large cardboard cylindrical tube four or five inches in diameter, with the company name Graffix printed all over it. Honestly, I didn't want my parents to see it, either. My parents are the most amazing people on this planet and have given me more than I have deserved, and I didn't want them to see the five-footer and worry. After all, we *did* graduate and that silly college partying was out of our systems. I think.

I had an epiphany one day and decided to take Sleepy to my brother's house, which he was renting at the time. And if it wasn't already, this house became the party house for those of us who refused to let the college party days die, even after we had graduated. So, yes, I had three more years of nonstop parties. Great success!

After my brother was evicted from this party house, which came to be known as The Zion Road House (topic for another book) in Bargaintown, New Jersey, Sleepy was homeless. I took it upon myself to store it in my parent's basement at their home. My thinking was that if I put the bong in the cardboard container and placed it up in the basement rafters by the fishing poles, it would blend in, and my parents might never see it until I had the chance to relocate it. And if they did happen to see it, they might think it was some type of fishing equipment. I mean, how often would you open up a long cardboard cylinder next to the fishing poles to see what was inside?

A year went by and my father was in the basement and decided to do a little organizing and move some storage items around. He came across the five-footer.

Now, my parents didn't even drink alcohol nor did they ever touch an illegal drug in their lives. They are, however, well-educated and had learned enough to know what a bong was, but there was no way in hell that my dad would ever suspect a bong could be five feet in length.

I remember walking down into the basement and my dad going over, pointing to the cardboard cylinder, and asking what it was. *Blame your brother, blame your brother*, a little voice inside my head was saying. It was always better to lie and live to see another day then plan an operation for the extraction of this device from the basement. "Oh, that's my brother's. I think it's a boat antenna or something . . . murmur, murmur, murmur." It worked. He placed it gently to the side until he could find a better place for such a delicate boating instrument.

Over the next year, my dad reorganized the basement a few more times and moved the "boat antenna" from point A to point B, and I even think he put it in a special rack so as not to disturb it.

Then catastrophe hit my dad's basement—his workshop and sanctuary. An invasion of furniture bugs got into everything and ruined the boxes of many stored treasures. My parents had to order one of those big rollaway dumpsters, empty the contents of the basement, and throw away the inexpensive items. It was time to open the cardboard tube and assess the antenna's value.

Oops! My dad was in shock that someone would make a "marijuana pipe," as he called it, so long in length. We were all busted.

Years later, when my parents realized that pot smoking was just a growing-up phase, we all had a big laugh at the story. And yes, it was a phase. We don't smoke pot anymore and my brother is a very successful union carpenter. Our friends from the Zion Road House went on to become doctors, lawyers, business owners, politicians, police officers, and teachers.

"What are you doing on my boat?"

The year was 2001. It was a hot summer in Destin, Florida, and many strange alignments occurred that led me there.

There used to be a restaurant and bar called Harry T's located right on Highway 98 in Destin. I was told to call the bar manager in early spring about a potential job as a bartender. A friend of mine from Washington, DC, had given me a great recommendation to the bar manager. I had also just finished up a winter season at Copper Mountain, Colorado, and one of the servers spent her summers in Destin and also knew the bar manager. I was hired over the phone.

What a summer that was. That place had to be one of the most exciting and busiest places I had ever worked. I ended up moving in with some coworkers from the restaurant that was a few miles away by car. Harry T's was situated on the bay on the Intracoastal Waterway. There was a harbor behind the restaurant that looked out toward a peninsula called Holiday Isle. That was where we lived for the summer—across the bay on the peninsula. If one were to swim, it would be a little over a half mile from where we lived.

That was exactly what our dumb drunk antics led us to do. After working a busy shift at the restaurant, my coworkers and I were in the habit of having a few after work drinks and then going barhopping.

One night after an evening of heavy drinking, the kitchen manager, also my roommate, decided that he was going to swim home from Harry T's, all the way home to Holiday Isle peninsula. He made it home. No problem. A few nights after this drunken swim-a-thon, I was at Harry T's having some cocktails with coworkers and a gaggle of women. That was when I started saying to myself that if the kitchen manager could swim home, so could I.

Now, I am a decent swimmer. After all, I was a lifeguard on the South Jersey shore for eleven summers. However, after drinking what I drank that night, I could barely walk. So here is a word of advice. If you are too drunk to walk, do not swim.

I stripped down to my boxer shorts, placed my clothes, wallet, and keys on the wheel of my car in the parking lot, and proceeded to the end of the dock. I vaguely remember a coworker and a few girls accompanying me toward the edge of the dock. They were all pleading with me not to do this because I was too drunk, which in my mind was more of a challenge.

Splash. And I was off! I was swimming. And swimming. And swimming. Gradually, I swam slower. And slower. Then I did the sidestroke. After about twenty minutes, barely even close to the middle, I was exhausted. I could barely see the lights of the peninsula. I tried to touch bottom to catch my breath. Not a good idea as my head completely submerged, and I began to choke and cough up the nasty bay water. All around was total darkness, black skies with no stars, and an even scarier shade of black in the water.

At this point, I had a sober moment and thought to myself, *I am going under. I am too drunk, and I can't make it.* Just then, off to my left, I saw a big boat moored to some floating buoys. With every last bit of energy, I swam to the boat, climbed up to catch my breath, and saved myself from tomorrow's headlines. I must have made the loudest noises trying to heave myself up onto that big boat. Suddenly, all the lights on the boat turned on. What I didn't know was that it was a houseboat anchored in the middle of the harbor.

Here came this guy running at me as I was gasping for breath and trying to explain that I was dying out there. My boxer shorts were hanging down past my knees as I realized he was not listening, and he began to chase me with either an umbrella pole or a broom handle. I was not too sure what he had in his hands. All I knew was that it was going to hurt when he hit me with it. He was also yelling to his wife, "Honey, call the coast guard! Call the coast guard!"

Out of the corner of my eye, I saw Honey with a phone the size of a military device phoning the troops. I somehow shucked and jived past all this mayhem and ran towards the bow of the boat. I remember yelling something back like, "I am out of here, you guys are mean!" And with that, I launched into a swan dive to splash back into the bay. I jumped high in the air with both arms back and a perfect back arch. I swear I could have earned a 9.5 in the Olympics with this swan dive. Splat!

It wasn't the bow of the boat. It was the stern. And when I dove off, I only succeeded in landing on the lower deck on the bait wells. At that point I was wincing in pain and the couple had stopped chasing me and stopped calling for help as they watched me in disbelief. I rolled over about twenty times and finally splashed into the water where I resumed my death swim.

Don't ask me how, but thirty minutes after interrupting this poor couple's relaxing slumber, I made it to where I could touch bottom. I must have over-swam my destination by about six blocks, because I found myself running down the street thinking the military was coming to take me away. Looking back on the road, all I saw was wet footprints and heard the sound of splashing as I ran with bare feet to the back door of our apartment.

After about twelve hours of sleep, I woke up naked and sore as hell. Every muscle in my body ached and throbbed with tightness and soreness. A few weeks later, I heard a story from one of the day bartenders at Harry T's that the house-boat couple had been in having lunch and had recounted the horror story of how a crazy, maniac pirate swam out to their boat in the middle of the harbor at 2:00 a.m., woke them up, and did a swan dive onto the lower deck. In my defense, the bartender had said something like, "Oh my God, that was Johnny. He is harmless. He just decided to swim home and almost died."

So here's a prime example of how booze made me feel like Michael Phelps and led me to bad and dangerous decisions.

Lessons Learned?

So I have had my share of growing pains making risky decisions with both substances. I have tried to learn from these crazy experiences. Thank goodness they didn't turn out disastrous. I tell the stories lightly, but my humor is also a justification mechanism. Weed and alcohol can both be dangerous and, for me, alcohol is the bigger evil. I see so many others, every week, who seem to experience weed and alcohol the same way as I do, with insanity and bad judgment heavy on the alcohol side. Like I said, you can make yourself crazy researching the ever-changing studies, but I do find the following resources helpful.

- www.RecoveryFirst.org/Alcohol-vs-Marijuana.html
- www.DrugFreeworld.org/DrugFacts/Marijuana.html
- www.LiveScience.com/42738-Marijuana-vs-Alcohol-Health-Effects.html

CHAPTER 13

A World Weedgalized

During the first year of legalization, Colorado's culture changed in a variety of ways. I noticed an increase in population, many unique new businesses and jobs in the cannabis industry, and an overall sense of acceptance of the new laws. As a bartender, I still get asked several times per week, "Where is the closest dispensary?" In this chapter are some cultural shifts and new events legal pot spawned during the first year.

Marijuana Job Fair

Yes, there is such a thing as a marijuana job fair. During the first year of legalization, several fairs were held during the spring of 2014 in the Denver area. These fairs were well attended. I guess it's no secret that people were and are eager to take advantage of this budding new industry. Jobs posted at the fairs included copywriters, graphic designers, tour guides, web developers, budtenders, trimmers, growers, pot event planning, security, extraction technicians, dispensary managers, marketing, delivery drivers, solar panel specialists, horticulturalists, lawyers, teachers of new courses on marijuana law, marijuana journalist, edibles producer, packaging, labeling, brand managers, and strain reviewers. Waits of two or more hours to get into the fairs were common.

Banking

Many stores and shops, if not all, were concerned early on that they could not use the banking system, since marijuana is still illegal on the federal level. At the time I write this, in mid-2015, the issue remains. Banks fear any backlash from the federal government by accepting and insuring money from the cannabis industry. This means that they are an all-cash business. Thus they are at risk of being robbed, and the safety and welfare of employees are threatened. I have since seen the use of debit cards in a few dispensaries I have visited.

I keep hearing about efforts from many private corporations to create Colorado-based credit unions that will enable the industry to use a banking system, but nothing has yet been confirmed or implemented.

Ever-changing Policies: A Work in Progress

As Colorado was the first in the nation to undertake such an endeavor, officials repeatedly said it is "a work in progress." The following article was published in our local newspaper, *Grand Junction Free Press*, on September 29, 2014, and reprinted here courtesy of Rocky Mountain PBS I-News. I reprint it here to provide a snapshot of the complexities new marijuana businesses faced during that roller-coaster first year, in a world where rules changed by the minute.

"Colorado's Marijuana Enforcement Division releases new rules for medical, retail marijuana businesses"

Medical and retail marijuana dispensaries will receive about 30 new rules related to almost every aspect of their businesses.

The state's Marijuana Enforcement Division (MED) released the new rules Thursday, September 24, 2014. They change everything from the start up licensing fees, to rules for cultivation, production, edibles, sales, employee training, and product testing. Right down to a hand washing requirement.

State officials have contended that Colorado's new recreational marijuana industry is a work in progress, and these new standards underscore that fact.

"I think the new rules make a lot of sense," said Mark Slaugh, CEO of iComply, a cannabis industry compliance and consulting firm. "We're putting out consumer education and teaching business owners and workers how to be responsible vendors. From a business decision, it's a no brainer."

Among the new rules is a revision of a proposal that caused an uproar at a hearing earlier this month— production caps on greenhouse or outdoor grows.

The proposed rule would have allowed greenhouses to produce only half the amount of plants allowed at indoor or warehouse operations. The new rules do not make that distinction and allow the same number of plants, 3,600, for the first level cultivation process.

"I think that the state really listened to the greenhouse workers and was responsive to the impassioned testimony," said Meg Collins, executive director of the Cannabis Business Association, and one member of the work group committee writing the production rules. In the new rules, the enforcement division also established minimum "responsible vendor training" requirements, along with minimum public health and safety requirements for anyone manufacturing edible marijuana products.

The state has issued 18,666 marijuana occupational licenses as of 2014. Each individual with a license will be required to meet new minimum training standards if hired by a shop, cultivation center, testing facility, or product manufacturer. There are approximately 500 licensed medical shops and another few hundred recreational stores in Colorado. The state has received 177 additional applications for recreational stores and grow operations that could be approved by the date of October 1, 2014. These numbers will change but it gives you an idea of how much and how fast the industry is growing.

Aside from safety and health training, new rules will also normalize the amount of marijuana found in any edible — ensuring that a single serving size has no more than 10 milligrams of active THC, the intoxicating chemical in marijuana.

"So that could be something as small as a peanut butter cup or bonbon or as large as a soda," said iComply's Slaugh. "If there is more than one serving in the product, it has to be easily identified."

The serving size rule is meant to ensure a more safe consumption of edible marijuana. Edibles have a greater risk for over consumption because the digestion of marijuana causes a later onset of the effects. Some people respond by eating more.

Testing requirements have also changed. MED will not only require testing for potency in edibles, but also for chemicals like pesticides and for the presence of fungi. "I already spend a small fortune every month testing and that is only going up because of all the other things they are testing," Ruden said. "I'm excited for more responsible regulation, but frustrated with the expenses, the licensing fees, taxes, and testing."

Others expressed concern with what the new rules don't include.

Marijuana testing facilities will only test product from licensed cultivation centers, not home growers or medical marijuana caregivers.

"We're still not able to know how to dose," said Ashley Weber, medical marijuana patient and caregiver advocate. "From a caregiver's side, not being able to test means you don't know what you're giving your patient and you are never going to be able to be on a consistent level. And for parents with kids with epilepsy, (they) can't know if they are overmedicating their children (or) when (to) give the medication."

MED has not yet considered expanding testing services to caregivers.

Others were concerned that the mass of new regulations might mean more costs, and continuing competitions from the black or gray markets.

"The more rules you have the more challenging it is because we are driving up the price," Slaugh said. "We can offer a consistent, safe product and a wider variety and you don't have to deal with a drug dealer—I think legitimate market will always drive away the black market—except for the price." [29]

Graffiti on Bathroom Wall in Idaho Springs

On a trip to Denver, I stopped to use a restroom in Idaho Springs. Written on the wall was, "Smoke Responsibly. Keep Colorado Green." That's an example of Colorado weed smokers trying to keep a respectable control of the legalized weed that still carries a social stigma. Perhaps graffiti is not the best medium for a message, but it is an attempt to convey a popular sentiment nonetheless.

Thrift Store Response to Legalization via Creative Disclaimer Signage

There is a thrift store located close to a dispensary up here in Summit County. Inside the store there is the funniest disclaimer posted on the wall. The sign reads, "Due to the organic nature of the medical marijuana dispensaries located adjacent to our store, Summit Thrift and Treasure may incur a skunky smell from time to time." I couldn't help but chuckle quietly to myself because I could smell it.

> *Due to the organic nature of the medical marijuana dispensaries located adjacent to our store, Summit Thrift and Treasure may incur a skunky smell from time to time*

I decided to ask some of the staff what the story was behind the sign. They chuckled as well and explained that since the dispensaries actually grow a portion of their product on site, the smell that comes over sometimes is from the actual growing operation. "Sometimes we can smell it on people who go shopping at the dispensary first, then come to the thrift shop. Surprisingly, it's often the polite elderly folks."

Slate Magazine's Funny Story (August 24, 2014)

Colorado has never chosen an official state dessert. Most states have a dessert, like New York has the cheesecake, New Jersey has saltwater taffy, Georgia has peach cobbler, Florida has key lime pie. So *Slate Magazine* suggested that pot candy or pot brownies be the state dessert. Nothing official has come out in response. Which type of edible could be chosen as Colorado's official dessert? Pot brownie, pot cookie, gummy bears? This remains to be seen.[30]

Researching the Benefits of Medical Marijuana

In 2015, Colorado will release $8 million from medical marijuana patient fees to study the potential of medical uses of marijuana. The fees will cover grants awarded by the Colorado Board of Health to study various conditions and illnesses such as: arthritis, childhood epilepsy, brain tumors, bone degeneration, Parkinson's disease, and PTSD (post-traumatic stress disorder). This is a landmark study since most of the prior studies focused mainly on the negative aspects of marijuana.[31]

Feds Pass Law Granting Legalization of Marijuana on Reservation Lands

Native American tribes on reservations land may cultivate and sell marijuana regardless of state laws. This news was released on Thursday, December 11, 2014:

> "Finally, Native Americans are really beginning to experience true sovereignty," said Dan Skye, editor-in-chief of *HIGH TIMES*. "Cannabis—whether it's industrial hemp, medical, or recreational marijuana—can provide employment and economic stimulus on Indian reservations, which is so desperately needed."[32]

Pot Critics

There do exist pot critics who taste, smoke, and critique marijuana strains. Inquisitive cannabis consumers can find reviews of various types of pot on *The Denver Post's* "The Cannabist" blog as well as on *The Cannabis Connoisseur Connection* (YouTube Series at www.YouTube.com/watch?v=AViPrXzJoDg) and www.THCFarmer.com/Community.

Pot Stocks

"Pot stocks? Really? What do you mean *pot stocks*? Do you mean there are marijuana companies listed? Like in the Dow Jones?" Yep.

That was pretty much how a conversation at the bar went one night with a guest who couldn't comprehend that many companies dealing in some aspect of the marijuana industry are listed on the stock exchange. There's even a whole website dedicated to marijuana stocks at www.MarijuanaStocks.com.

Another gentleman was having dinner when a pot discussion broke out, as they tend to do often. This guy works in the commercial real estate industry in the Denver area. He chimed in that he bought some pot stocks back in January 2014, had already sold them by the end of February, and tripled a large chunk of his portfolio in sixty days. Almost all marijuana stocks shot up in value around January and February of 2014. Some rose as high as one hundred times their value. Most of those have come back down since then.

The stocks that Karpy and I like have the following ticker symbols: PHOT, MJNA, and HEMP. HEMP has been around the longest and has a huge upside potential if the hemp industry takes off. Their public company was at the Cannabis Capital Summit in Denver in 2014 displaying a large wall of accolades and awards.

There are ads on Craigslist from the first year inviting one to send away for marijuana stock info. I found one and sent in my address and received this postcard in the mail:

The original postcard was in a beautiful cannabis green color.

CHAPTER 14

Top Ten Questions:
YEAR ONE

During the first year of legalization, I got asked the same questions so often I decided to create a "Top Ten" list. Without further ado, here's the Johnny Bartender Top Ten list. I'll list the answers I gave at that time to give you a snapshot of those days, and then I'll update the answers as of the writing of this book.

Johnny Bartender's
Top Ten Cannabis Questions

1. Where is the closest dispensary?

2. Do you think this will bring a lot of people to the state of Colorado?

3. Where can we smoke?

4. Have you seen a change in people?

5. Do you know of any jobs that I can get clipping and pruning marijuana plants?

6. What effect will this have on the old marijuana dealers—the black market, so to speak?

7. Is marijuana any cheaper now?

8. If marijuana is legal now, what happens if my company has a drug policy in place prohibiting marijuana use?

9. What states are next?

10. How can you write a book on marijuana if you don't even smoke?

Johnny Bartender's Answers: Then and Now

1. Where is the closest dispensary?

Then: If you're in my bar, pretty much around the corner.

Now: Ditto.

2. Do you think this will bring a lot of people to Colorado?

Then: Yes, I have already seen a steady influx of people coming to this state for the past several years due to this industry. Keep in mind medical marijuana has been here since 2009. Even before it was on the ballot, many entrepreneurs were moving in and setting up shop. I personally put an ad on Craigslist for a roommate about two years ago, and a young man from Florida responded. He was an entrepreneur, ambitious, and a grower of cannabis. In the past year I have met and served dinner and drinks to many guys and gals that are starting up new businesses and have already created jobs—the *ganjapreneurs.*

Then I get the people who come in with the giggles who can't believe that this day is finally here. They are the ones who are here out of curiosity and almost a state of disbelief.

I even heard a rumor of a company in our neighboring state of Kansas. The company is offering bus tours to go across the state line into Colorado so that the customers can purchase and smoke and then get a ride back. Of course they are smoking it all and bringing nothing back to the state of Kansas.

There are similar companies in Colorado. One is profiled in Chapter 4 of this book. It is called Cultivating Spirits. The customers pay a fee for a safe ride around town to all the dispensaries on a given list and the ride is a limousine.

Now: More than a year has passed since regulation, and at the bar I still hear from tourists and locals alike that they feel that this state has exploded with tourism and population increases. When I ask what they see as the cause, I hear "marijuana legislation" almost 100 percent of the time. So from what I've learned behind the bar, anyway, legalization has helped bring many people to the state.

I came across an article in which the title says it all: "Pot-friendly Denver saw a 73 PER CENT increase in hotel searches since last year as Easter weekend falls on April 20, the nation's unofficial marijuana holiday."[33]

3. Where is it safe to smoke?

Then: This is a great question, because it demonstrates a little respect. Be sure to check with the updated list of rules and regulations in any town that you may visit. Before marijuana was legal, I would see people smoking pot in parking lots, chairlifts, alleyways, and campgrounds. Now that it is legal, I see less and less of this. People are aware there are new rules, and there are more eyes looking. Yes, you may purchase marijuana, but you may not consume it in public places. I tell people to smoke in the privacy of their own homes. Yes, it may be legal to purchase now, but keep it on the down low. I will repeat and translate that. Keep it on the down low; translated as do not advertise your smoking or the "award-winning aroma" of your strain, because there are still a great many folks who oppose it. Don't give them any additional reasons to try to impose more laws or start a new lobby group. Plain and simple, don't give anyone a reason to hate the players or the game.

While at work, I witnessed two gals allegedly smoking a bowl in a public place. Every guest who was at the bar at that time allegedly smelled the same distinct smell that I smelled. I walked over to them and said, "Just in case you are wondering and just in case that may be the newly legalized substance in Colorado, please do not smoke that in public. It is better to smoke anything like that in the privacy of your own home." The two gals looked at me and apologized immediately, put the alleged marijuana bowl away, and gave me a smile. Again, it's best to show the utmost respect to those whom oppose marijuana's recreational use.

Refer to the website www.Colorado.gov where there is a current list of the state's laws. If in doubt, contact your local authorities for clarification of the rules. Again, don't assume on your own and say, "Oh, Johnny the bartender said otherwise!"

Now: Not much has changed, but there is a feeling that more locals and tourists are learning the rules and laws about where to smoke.

4. Have you seen a change in restaurant customers?

Then: Yes, some customers seem more relaxed, content, and happier. This is my observation, anyway.

I did hear a negative story about some of the customers waiting in line at the dispensaries. A young doctor-to-be was telling me that she had a bad experience due to some ignorant folks waiting in line and not wanting to wait their turn.

Now: Still happy!

5. Do you know of any jobs that I can get clipping and pruning marijuana plants?

Then: I did know of many positions available in the first year from the local dispensary owners that I interviewed. I heard of even more in the Denver area. I began to meet many folks new to the area who work in this industry.

Now: The word that I hear around town and from those in the cannabis industry is that there are still many jobs available in the industry. There is turnover in the cannabis industry the same as might be found in the food and beverage industry or the ski industry.

6. What effect will this have on the old marijuana dealers, the black market so to speak?

Then: As you can read in detail in my interview with Anonymous Dealer in Chapter 9, "The Sellers," (See page 98), I believe black market dealers have been hurt by the legislation and are being driven out of business. As this is one of the reasons for the legislation, I have to say that's a good thing, although I do feel bad for the dealers I've met personally.

Now: More than a year after legalization, most of the local dealers I knew have gone into other lines of work, or into other states.

7. Now that it is legal, is marijuana any cheaper?

Then: Allow me to translate this for the general public. What they are asking is whether it is cheaper now that it is in a store as opposed to the good old days where one could just "call the guy." The answer is no, it is not cheaper. In fact, I have heard that it is more expensive. However, I will say that while exploring dispensaries for this book, I found that purchasing marijuana is an experience unto itself. It could be argued that some may be looking for a social outlet when going to a dispensary, hoping to meet some fellow tokers.

Another observation of mine is that I have never seen a happier group of employees who are so enthused and knowledgeable about the product. I walk in, I'm greeted by all smiles, and they are all too eager to have me smell the various strains and tell me the unique and obscure names of each. These employees, as busy as they are, are so willing to chat. And believe me, when I visited the many dispensaries, the front entrance is like a revolving door with happy customers leaving and new ones entering or waiting to enter.

Sometimes when bar customers ask me if pot is cheaper or more convenient now, I tell them this joke. "I don't get it. It's not more convenient. Back in the day, I used to just 'call the guy,' and he would show up to my house or anywhere and bring me my weed. Now, I have to go get in line and choose from hundreds of kinds. Oh woe is me, decisions, decisions." Everyone laughs.

Now: As the market settles down, prices seem to fluctuate with demand and availability just as with any other product. Lines have shortened as people have become accustomed to shopping hours.

8. **If marijuana is legal now, what happens if my company has a drug policy in place prohibiting marijuana use?**

Then: I personally wouldn't risk it if my company or employer has a policy in place banning certain substances. Don't do it.

Now: Ditto.

9. **What states are next?**

Then: Any state could attempt to legalize and have it pass or not, so it is hard to say. Not to mention the fact that I'm a bartender, not a soothsayer or a reporter. This question always amuses me—people seem to think because I live in Colorado, I'm an expert on the legalization of pot around the country. Many of my friends have the same experience.

Now: Ditto!

10. How can you write a book about marijuana if you don't even smoke?

Then and Now: Whether I smoke or not isn't really relevant to the book. I'm not writing about the experience of smoking weed; I'm sharing the tales I've heard and the lessons I've learned in my catbird seat as a bartender in Summit County during the first year of marijuana legalization in Colorado. I am a storyteller, and this is a story of the first state in America to experience these new experiences. It is only the surface of a story of this size. This is not just a stoner's story; it's a Colorado and national story. These are unprecedented times for our country.

CHAPTER 15

Tidbits & Nuggets

CELEBRATING COLORADO'S CHOICES
A PRE-420 COMEDY AND MUSIC EVENT
AT **BARKLEY'S BALLROOM, IN FRISCO**

Featuring:

40oz TO FREEDOM
SUBLIMES BEST COVER BAND

Comedy Show by:

NGAIO BEALUM
APRIL 18 | DOORS OPEN @ 9PM
$10 PRE-SALE | $13 AT THE DOOR
GIVEAWAYS AND PRIZES THROUGHOUT THE NIGHT

"I was actually embarrassed it had taken me this long to get to Colorado. Of all the writers I know—really, of all the humans I know—I'm the biggest, most fervent, most frequent stoner. So it's beyond pathetic that it took me a year to get to the Holy Land, especially because I have the time. All summer, I sat around and said, 'I really should head up to Colorado for a couple of weeks.' And I could have done it, at pretty much any time.

"But instead, I just sat back and watched as unqualified CNN reporters (www.TheCannabist.co/tag/CNN/) got their tours of airplane hangars full of marijuana plants, as Dr. Sanjay Gupta, of all people (www.TheCannabist.co/2014/05/13/Changing-Tide-Drs-Gupta-Oz-Bessner-Changed-Minds-Medical-Pot/11705/), became pot's biggest advocate.

"For Marley's sake, Maureen Dowd (www.TheCannabist.co/tag/Maureen-Dowd/) went to Denver and got high before me, and she is not qualified (www.TheCannabist.co/2014/06/04/New-York-Times-Dowd-Marijuana-Edibles-Became-Convinced-Died-One-Telling/13036/). I was missing the revolution.

"Finally, I could wait no longer. The last person to the party still gets to attend."

—Neal Pollack (author of eight books
and three-time *Jeopardy* winner)[34]

Illustration by Mariah Hildreth

A Johnny Bartender Observation

Neal Pollack's quote really is how a lot of people feel about the legalization of cannabis. It is like a pilgrimage to a holy land for those who truly believe in the medical and healing properties of the plant.

Liquor Sales Rep Travel Story

Here's what it is like for Coloradoans when travelling. There's a good friend who lives up here in the mountains and is a liquor sales rep for a big company. Every time she travels out of state, she brings back stories. While in Mexico on a tour bus, the tour guide asked everyone where they came from. When she said Colorado, everyone turned to look and began asking questions. "So what's it like over there?" "Did you bring any of the good stuff?" Even a cop from Chicago asked about the weed in Colorado. Another time she was in Fort Meyers, Florida, and she met a little old lady of about eighty years, who asked my friend if she brought over any of the good "hooch." Of course, my friend didn't bring any out of state. And finally, when she was at Denver International Airport she met a bunch of guys from Austin, Texas. They began to describe their whole Colorado experience by saying that they came for three days to try the marijuana. They ended up spending all three days in their hotel room because they were so high. This scenario has played out for most of the Colorado residents that I have spoken to at the bar, especially those who have travelled out of the country.

High Altitude Bike Ride or Is It High Attitude?

One day a friend came into the bar talking about how she rode her bike around beautiful Lake Dillon near Frisco. It's actually a reservoir, and it is over twenty miles in circumference. Sitting at an elevation of over 9000 feet above sea level, this lake ride is not easy for most folks. It helps to be in pretty decent shape to accomplish this. After her ride, she went over to the local dispensary to purchase a small amount of pot. But she only had ten dollars. As she entered the dispensary, they asked if they could help her.

"I'm here to shop." But the smallest amount of the type she liked cost eighteen dollars.

"Damn, I only have ten dollars."

Another gal in the shop overheard this, turned, and gave my friend the difference she needed to make the purchase. The employees mentioned that they love when this type of good vibe happens in the store, and it happens all the time.

Friends Visiting from Out of State

During the first year of legalization, some friends from out of state came to visit the Colorado ski resorts. I got the funniest phone call from them when they arrived and were driving up to the mountain areas, about two hours from the airport. They called to tell me that they were in the rental car driving up, but before they got on the highway, they went from the airport to the nearest dispensary. So from the time the airplane touched down to the arrival at the dispensary, a whole forty-three minutes had passed. They stocked up on edibles and extracts and headed on up. Needless to say, it was a week of "high" adventure and extreme laughter. After their week stay, whatever they didn't consume was graciously donated to their favorite bartender in the mountains.

Pandora Radio and Pot

Here in Colorado there are now marijuana commercials on Pandora® Radio streaming music. The advertisements promote safe consumption of marijuana in the state of Colorado. The ads also say something like, "for visitors who don't consume, there is still plenty to do." I thought that last part was pretty funny.[35]

License Plate Profiling

News stories have been circulating that if you have a Colorado license plate on your vehicle and are traveling across state line, there's a higher chance of being pulled over by the police.

My brother, Charlie, moved from New Jersey to Colorado in 1995. He has driven across country over two hundred times from 1995 to 2013. After the legalization of marijuana in Colorado, sometime in 2014 he was making the usual trip across country with his wife, Shawn, and their new puppy.

Charlie was in the back of the suburban sleeping while Shawn drove the day shift. Around 10 a.m., they were pulled over for allegedly following a tractor trailer too close. Charlie woke up. The cops pulled him out of the car and placed him in the back of the police car. A forty-five minute interrogation ensued.

"Here's the problem I have, your eyes are all red."

"I was sleeping in the backseat. You just woke me up."

"Do you smoke pot?"

"No, I do not."

"Where are you heading? You from Colorado?"

"We are going to New Jersey. We have a house in both states."

"How do you have the means to own a house in both states?"

No comment from my brother but he was thinking, *Nunya*. (Jersey talk for, "None of your damn business.")

The cop changed his line of questioning and began asking questions about the dog. Apparently the cop was now suspicious about the puppy. My brother decided to ask why the dog was such a big deal.

"It's a good place to hide narcotics."

Now he was thinking, *Really*, but not in an inquisitive way.

"So what do you think about the legalization of marijuana?"

"To be honest, I don't care either way, it doesn't affect me. I'm a carpenter and I don't smoke pot."

The cop sent them on their way with a warning.

After fifteen minutes of driving he was pulled over by different cops again. Damn those Colorado license plates.

Hash Oil Explosions on the Rise

The attraction of getting a more potent high has been the cause of escalating hash oil explosions. Hash oil explosions, which are caused by butane tanks igniting, have been on the rise since the legalization of cannabis in 2014. The fact that adults over twenty-one can legally grow up to six plants in their homes might have led to increased experiments with hash oil extractions. Some law enforcement officials feel that this is a consequence of the legalization of marijuana. In 2013, there were twelve such explosions compared to thirty-two in 2014, the year of legalization.[36]

Hash oil is extracted from cannabis in a complex process that involves blasting it with butane. In an uncontrolled or unregulated operation, this process is dangerous and can explode in an instant. It's a serious cause for concern in residential areas, especially high-density areas like condos or apartment buildings. Law enforcement and fire officials are scrambling to solve this issue and reduce the number of these explosions. This can be viewed as one of the drawbacks of legalizing marijuana. There is a bill in legislation now that will make it a felony to use explosive gases like butane to manufacture hash oil inside a home or similarly confined space.

The CBD Oil and Epilepsy Story

Throughout my interviews with various dispensary owners, I have repeatedly heard stories about the use of CBD oil and childhood epilepsy. CBD stands for Cannabidiol, a cannabinoid from cannabis that can be extracted and made into oil. There are no psychoactive ingredients in this form, and it will not produce a high. Here is an excerpt from one of the many articles on this topic from CBS 4 in Denver released on November 18, 2013:

> There's a new strain of marijuana that has desperate parents full of hope. It won't get people high but they believe it provides relief for children suffering from seizures.
>
> It's about a five-step process to go from the plant to a thick, black liquid. It looks a bit like molasses but to a growing number of children it's simply good medicine.[37]

The reports are that this CBD oil curtails or stops epileptic seizures in children. This topic is so hot and so emotional that legislation for this alone is proposed in the United States Senate. Here is an excerpt from Epilepsy Foundation COLORADO:

> ### "CARERS Act Introduced in the Senate"
>
> Senators Cory Booker (NJ), Rand Paul (KY), and Kirsten Gillibrand (NY), have introduced legislation to move cannabis to Schedule II and to remove cannabidiol (CBD) from the Controlled Substances Act. The Compassionate Access, Research Expansion and Respect States (CARERS) Act (S. 683) would lift federal barriers to research on cannabis and CBD, and protect individuals in states with medical cannabis programs. Medical use of cannabis has been legalized in 23 states and the District of Columbia, and people

living with uncontrolled seizures have reported bene-
ficial effects and reduced seizure activity when using
medical cannabis, especially CBD oil.[38]

Black Friday Deals at Dispensaries

It was funny and strange to see and hear advertisements for
pot sales on Black Friday that first year. There was everything
from dollar joints to "buy one get one free" grams of the
"weed of the week." It's not just for retailers of clothes, toys,
and electronics anymore!

Marijuana Board

In addition to the Liquor Board within the Frisco town council,
there is now a Marijuana Board. This board oversees license
renewals for dispensaries as well as any other issues surrounding marijuana.

Animation Series Being Developed

My friend Chris Hoover, who helped me with this book, is
now working on an animation series. "In a nutshell," he said,
"I have a team of writers and artists working on an animated
series that is focused on the humor and the satirical appeal
the rapidly growing cannabis industry is in need of. There
are several hilarious characters that will be rising out of the
'mist' shortly." Chris is the author of *Imagine Freedom*.

First Year Gossip

During the first year of legalization, people came to some
pretty quick conclusions that I heard repeated all the time.

The research hadn't been done, but these five items were common knowledge—whether or not they were true.

1. Since the legalization of marijuana in Colorado, there is a noticeable increase in panhandlers and the homeless.

2. Since the legalization of marijuana in Colorado, there is a noticeable increase in tourism.

3. Since the legalization of marijuana in Colorado, the black market of illegal dealers has taken a big hit.

4. The majority of those who have been asked feel not much has really changed the first year.

5. The population of the state is rising.

Were they right? Here's what we know now:

1. **More panhandlers?** We see more of them at their favorite spots near traffic lights.

2. **More tourists?** I'm sure that if you ask any of the locals in our small town of Frisco they will say, "Yes." Those in the food and beverage industry might scream out the word, "Yes!"

3. **Black market sales?** Sales are still down from where they were in pre-legalization years. I'm guessing, as I have no way of knowing, since I don't buy illegal cannabis.

4. **Do people feel things haven't changed?** At first it did feel this way. Now that many small towns are

growing and Denver is as well, this sentiment seems to have changed.

5. **Is the population rising?** It is harder to cross or make a left turn on Main Street in our little town during busy months. The summer of 2015 has broken records for the number of cars coming up to Summit County through the Eisenhower Tunnel, according to town officials that have dinner at the restaurant. In my opinion, as a bartender, it feels like the population has doubled. A new theme that is now repeatedly shared on social media sites is that Colorado is full. One photo contains a play on words: it is of a sign that says, "Leaving 'ColorFULL' Colorado." Another website business, based in Colorado, is selling T-shirts that say, "Stop Moving to Colorado" and "You Got High, Now Go Home".

CHAPTER 16

The Future

The marijuana story is far from over. It is ever changing and never ending. I could keep writing each and every day due to the endless stories and new laws being created. Here is where we take a break and look ahead to years two and three unfolding.

There are so many variables in play in the current market such as banking, regulation of edibles, tax monies, and new legislation in many other states. It is hard to say what will happen first, since the state of Colorado is working on all simultaneously. According to Kristen Wyatt writing in the Associated Press, May 9, 2014, ideas for an uninsured financial cooperative have made some headway and may be a viable option for all the pot shops to use as a banking system.

Colorado has gone to work every day since 2014 to ensure we don't screw this whole thing up and look bad in the eyes of the world. For now, it is still so much fun to travel. When traveling and people hear that we are from Colorado, they begin to giggle. I'll tell you, it is quite the icebreaker.

Several questions will be answered in the next few years. How many other states will go to full legalization? Will the federal government reschedule marijuana so that it is not in the same class as cocaine and heroin? What will new research discover? Stay tuned.

Just like the Sheriff said, "We will see in fifty years if this was a good decision or not."

Acknowledgments

I want to thank the following people for being there with their talents to contribute and make this book a reality. Some have shared some links online, some have contributed information, some were integral parts of the equation, and some were just there to listen to me bounce my crazy ideas off them and that was a big help. Every word of encouragement that I received helped me to complete this project. Those listed below helped in some way with the creation of words on a page that turned into a literary project created by myself. This acknowledgment in no way connects them to cannabis or the industry unless otherwise stated in the book. My aim is to give thanks without tarnishing their reputation.

June and Dr. John W. Welsh
Kristen Welsh
Charlie and Shawn Welsh
Alicia Alonzo, for her love and unwavering support and for putting up with me pecking away at the keyboard
Dale and Patricia Beard
Aunt Jan and Tad
Johanna Hietala, for introducing me to the publishing world
Jody Rein, for her guidance and knowledge
Stephen Karp, for idea swapping sessions and contributions
Chris Hoover, for his insight and support
Macky Peter, for front cover design and artwork

Ryan Spencer, for cartoons in the book including
the burning joint series
Mariah Hildreth, for her artwork
Elle Mallone, for the opening cartoon of the U.S. map
and Colorado
Toni Knapp
Judith Briles and Author U.
Pam and Shawn Johnson
Ashley Greene
Kenneth Gonzalez
Craig Bernhardy
Sara Johnstone
Seth Zelen
Maria D. Spotts
Israel Bravo
Lindsay Wilson
Kristen Sheehan
Troy with graphic design
Jeremy Hodgeson
Brian Paonessa
Dan and Mirian Kibbie
Phil Wolf
Nick Brown
Ste-V Day
Brett Figeuroa
Greg Rando
Fred Colagiovanni
Allen Hollyfield
Jillian Turner
Jessica Catalano
Charles Stott
Lauren (Smiley) Stott

Rick and Judy Amico
Keith Hogan
Jonny Greco
Rob Saldano
Kim Wilson
Dominic Phillips
Casey Rodriguez
Jerry Olson
Karen and Lisa from The Next Page Bookstore
on Main St., Frisco, CO
Neal Bocksch
Dirk Fowler
Valerie Pipher
Kim Mauser
Angelique Justich
Matt Lee
The Campy's
Rich Dzomba and Florida Todd
John and Pat Chambers
Brenda and Andy
Kelli and Todd Mundt
Quincy and David Salem
John Minor
Kat King
Frank McDonald
Ricardo Baca
Neal Pollack
Mitch Dickman
Andrew Benton
Rhett Jordan
Lexi Borbotsina
Native Roots Frisco staff: Taylor, Eric, Joel

Matt Karukin

Kurt Kizer

Brendan Wakefield-Silves

Freddie Wyatt

Gilbert Ramos

Ray Villa

Amanda Tasty-Kakes

Tim and Michelle Putz

Nick Zelinger, NZ Graphics

Helena Mariposa

Kris Doubleday

Staff and coworkers: Krista Martinson, Natalie Ricks, Joe Bucholz, Carol Jedd, Victoria Salinas, Paige Lewis, Brandon Lund, Tim Exley, Zack Silverman, Kayla Alaimo, Meghan Nelson, AB, Mark Fenke, David, Flip, Gavin, Erik, Ben, Devon, Brogan, Larry, Sam, Cassie, Mark Fox, John Fayhee, Brad, Morgan, and Gray

I also need to give big thanks to my favorite authors who over the years have taught and inspired me: Jim Rohn, Earl Nightingale, Bill Phillips, Mark Victor Hansen, Brian Tracey, Tony Robbins, Jack Canfield, Tim Ferriss, Tucker Max, Chris and Janet Attwood, T. Harv Eker, and Dale Carnegie. The tools needed to write a book I found within the pages of their books and especially audiobooks.

Thank you to all the teachers of English, grammar, and writing that I had growing up, I heard your voices in my head when I was writing.

Again, I want to thank the Cultivating Spirits CEO, Philip Wolf, for his ingenuity and generosity, and a shout out of thanks to his partner, Nick Brown. And last but not least, thanks to the support staff including Chef Brandon, Reba, Angelique, Sara, Matt, and Shane.

Thank you to all the tourists, travelers, guests, and visitors that ventured into Colorado and had the curiosity to ask the questions that inspired this book. Frisco Family Forever.

Appendices

Appendix I

Dispensary Guide: A Tour of Colorado's Pot Holes

Here is an informal collection of some of the dispensaries to check out while in Colorado. My friends and customers have recommended these most often as their favorites. Check out the online list at www.WeedMaps.com for current list and contact information.

Native Roots
(Medical and recreational)
Locations everywhere. See www.NativeRoots303.com for information.

High Country Healing
(Recreational and medical)

High Country Healing II
See www.HighCountryHealing.com for locations in Colorado Springs, Silverthorne, and Alma.

Herbal Bliss
(Recreational and medical)
842 North Summit Blvd., #13, Frisco, CO 80443
Near the intersection of North Summit Blvd. and Ten Mile Dr.
970-668-3514

Medical Marijuana of the Rockies
720 North Summit Blvd., Suite 101a
Frisco, CO 80443
Between County Road 1040 and Hawn Dr.

970-668-6337
www.MMRockies.com

The Kine Mine
(Recreational and medical)
2820 Colorado Blvd.
Idaho Springs, CO 80452
303-567-2018
www.TheKineMine.com

Organix
(Recreational and medical)
1795 Airport Road
Breckenridge,CO 80424
www.MyOrganics.com

Mile High Recreational Cannabis
1705 Federal Blvd.
Denver, CO 80204
www.MHMCDenver.com

Breckenridge Organic Therapy
1900 Airport Rd, Suite A1
Breckenridge, CO, 80424
970-453-0420

Nature's Spirit
113 E. 7th Street
Leadville, CO 80461
719-486-1900
www.NaturesSpirit420.com

Green Man Cannabis
1355 Santa Fe Drive, Suite F
Denver, CO 80204

www.GreenManCannabis.com
720-842-4842

Denver Relief
(Medical and recreational)
1 Broadway #A150
Denver, CO 80203
303-420-6337
www.DenverRelief.com

iVita Wellness—Franklin
3980 Franklin St.
Denver, CO 80205
720-524-8273
www.iVitaWellness.com

Frosted Leaf Federal
445 Federal Blvd.
Denver, CO 80204
303-355-4372
See www.FrostedLeaf.com for other locations.

Terrapin Care Station
1795 Folsom Street
Boulder, CO 80302
303-954-8402
www.TerrapinCareStation.com

Green Dragon
(Medical and recreational)
1420 Devereux Rd.
Glenwood Springs, CO 81601
970-230-9057
www.GreenDragonColorado.com

The Green Joint

(Recreational)
1030 Grand Avenue
Glenwood Springs, CO 81601
970-384-1234
www.TheGreenJoint.com

The Dandelion

(Recreational)
845 Walnut St.
Boulder, CO 80302
303-459-4676
www.TheDandelionCo.com

Choice Organics

(Recreational)
813 Smithfield Dr. Unit B
Fort Collins, CO 80524
970-472-6337
www.ChoiceOrganicsInc.com

Maggie's Farm MMJ

Locations in Colorado Springs, Cañon City, and Pueblo
See www.MaggiesFarmMarijuana.com for information.

Medicine Man

4750 Nome St.
Denver, CO 80239
303-373-0752

1901 South Havana St.
Aurora, CO 80014
303-923-3825
www.MedicineManDenver.com

Euflora Recreational Marijuana
401 16th Street Mall
Denver 80202
See www.EufloraColorado.com for other locations.

For a current list of all medical and recreational dispensaries in Colorado, visit www.WeedMaps.com.

Contact www.Weedgalized.com to have your dispensary listed or a potential interview included in the next volume of Weedgalized.

Appendix II

Summit County District 5 Flyer

Here is the rules and regulations flyer about marijuana provided by the Frisco Police Station. Check your own town's local ordinances. They may not be the same as Frisco. Go to www.Colorado.gov for updates and current laws.

Marijuana Laws In Colorado

What's in the Law?

It is never legal to smoke marijuana in public. Therefore, it is not okay on a ski lift, parking lot, or inside a business. Inside your home is a private, legal place to smoke, but never around children.

Possession and Consumption

- Adults over twenty-one may possess up to one ounce of marijuana on their person. Possession under twenty-one is never legal.

- Possessing over one ounce of marijuana is a misdemeanor offense. Twelve ounces or more is a felony.

- Selling or giving to a person under age twenty-one is a serious felony offense.

- Driving while marijuana impaired is illegal. A person is assumed illegally affected by marijuana at very low doses—five nanograms per milliliter. Don't smoke and drive.

Buying and Growing

- Marijuana can only be purchased from a licensed store, called a dispensary. A license may be obtained only from the Colorado Department of Revenue, Marijuana Enforcement Division.

- Sales are taxed at a minimum rate of 25 percent by the state. Local taxes may also apply.

- Home cultivation must be done in compliance with local building codes and state restrictions.

- It is legal to grow up to six marijuana plants but the seventh may put a person in prison.

Four Corners of Colorado

- Marijuana legalization laws described here apply only in Colorado, not any other state.

- The federal government considers marijuana illegal. There are many places in the mountains of Colorado that are United States government property, such as National Forests. This includes ski areas.

- Marijuana may not be shipped or sent through the mail.

- Marijuana may not be taken across the Colorado border by car, on an airplane, or by any other means.

- Colorado sales to out-of state residents cannot exceed one-quarter ounce for a single transaction.

Your Local Town Can Ban Marijuana Dispensaries

Rights Require Responsibility:
Law Enforcement Message

Marijuana can be addictive and harmful. Marijuana smoke can cause respiratory problems, the same as tobacco, and marijuana usage during pregnancy can have serious consequences for a baby, including long-term learning deficits.

Marijuana can be addictive. If you, a friend, or a family member is at risk of addiction, reach out for help.[39]

Appendix III

Pot Stocks

Below is a small sample of some of the pot stocks I bought at the recommendation of some of my customers, to give you an idea of what companies are creating out there. I found these companies impressive enough to buy the stocks, but that's just me. I'm not recommending any of these stocks to you.

I feel I should repeat: this is not a full list and these are not recommendations. Do your homework and research, especially with penny stocks. I don't want to hear that you bought a stock and lost money, and then you say something like, "But my bartender said it was a good stock!"

American Green, Inc (ERBB)
www.AltitudeOrganic.com

BG Medical Technologies, Inc. (RIGH)
www.BGMedTech.com

Cannabis Science, Inc. (CBIS)
www.CannabisScience.com

CannaVEST Corp. (CANV)
www.CannaVest.com

Fusion Pharm, Inc. (FSPM)
www.FusionPharmInc.com

GreenGro Technologies, Inc. (GRNH)
www.GreenGroTech.com

Growlife, Inc. (PHOT)
www.GrowLifeInc.com

GW Pharmaceuticals PLC (GWPH)
www.GWPharm.com

Hemp, Inc. (HEMP)
www.HempInc.com

Medical Marijuana, Inc. (PINX: MJNA)
www.MedicalMarijuanaInc.com

MediSwipe, Inc (MWIP)
www.MediSwipe.com

Terra Tech Corp. (TRTC)
www.TerraTechCorp.com

Appendix IV

100 Nicknames for Marijuana by Stephen Karp

Submit your favorite or unique name on the website for a chance to be selected in future volumes (www.Weedgalized.com).

Afternoon Delight
AK47
Alaskan Dog Fuck
Art Supplies
Bhudda
Bob Marley
Bruce Banner
Bubonic chronic
Bud
Cannabis
Cannabis *Sativa*
Cheeba
Cheech and Chong
Chronic
Crippie
Cumbustible love
Dank
Demp
Devil's Lettuce
Diesel
Dime Bag Special
Doja
Doobie

Dope
Dragpo
Dro
Fallbrook redhair
Filler
Frankenstein
Fuente
Fun
Ganja
Gong
Goofy Boots
Grass
Green
Green Monster
Green Panties
Greenbud
Hash
Hemp
Herb
Hooch
Hungry Hungry Hippie
Hydro
Indian boy

Indo
Kali
KB
Krang
Kush
Laughing Grass
Left handed Cigarettes
Marijuana
Mary Jane
Maui Wowie
Mersh
Mids
Northern Lights
Nuggets
Nugs
Oscar The Grouch
Panama Red
Peacebloom
Peyote
Phillies
Pot
Prince Albert left handed can
puff
Puff puff Give
Puff the magic Dragon
Purple Haze
Purple Sticky Punch
Reefer
Resin

Scally Wag
Schwag
Shit
Shrubbery
Silver haze
Skunk
Smoke
Space Cowboy
Sticky Icky
Sustenance
Sweet Leaf
Sweet Thang
Tetrahydracannibal
THC
Trainwreck
Tumbleweed
Tweed
Vipe
wacky tabacky
Weed
White Widow
Wizzeed
Yoda

. . . that's why they call it dope.

Appendix V

Marijuana Strains

The List Goes On. Don't Strain Yourself by Stephen Karp

When it comes to our weedy little fun flower, some pretty intelligent folks are trying strain after strain and coming up with strain after strain in their fancy little gardens, to the point that…well, let's start with this list that just touches the tip of the iceberg. For all practical purposes, the list of cannabis strains is unlimited, never ending, and could possibly be infinite.

Along with the very creative given names, I'll try to outline and describe just why each strain has made its way on the list. Marijuana has been used for centuries for everything from a hangover to head banging headaches, or simply to enjoy a little down time with a good movie. Here is a starter list with which to have some fun. There are possibly over 25,000 different strains and growing!

Following are the more popular top twenty strains in the United States.

AFGAN HAZE

A strain running under a few different aliases, coming together in the early 2000s with a blend of Afghan and Haze with an earthy taste and a sweet metallic scent, this aggressive combo of Afghan female and Haze male creates a potent result.

Sense: happy, inspired, really hungry

LEMON THAI KUSH

Blended with Lemon Thai and OG Kush to create a balanced high. Has tropical scents and flavors, and a higher than normal percent of THC. When smoking, you'll notice woodsy flavors like pine, cedar, and a bunch of nature's natural flavors with hints of lemon and pepper. Through the nose you'll notice a citrus, lemony scent. Then an earthy, musky, woodsy smell will fill the room.

Sense: alert, anxious, energetic, happy, motivated, relaxed

M39

Drifted south from Canada in the early 1990s, born in Amsterdam, and combined with a Dutch commercial blend. Popular due to an easy to grow, fast to flower, high yielding plant. Used primarily within the medical community. This little leafy friend used to make its way into the United States in the saddle bags of biker gangs. Strange tastes related to this one. At first, asiago cheese with a hint of tangelo.

Sense: anxious, attentive, creative, energetic

YAABBA DABBA GOO

Introduced by "Cutting Edge Genetics" Enjoyed by pros and novices alike, a hybrid of California and Hawaiian culture. Loved by Washington and California folks alike for its fast growth and large flowers, giving it high status. Some consider this strain to be the best around. Like weed of the past with fruity tones, tangy and fruity nose.

Sense: energetic, euphoric, relaxed

OREGON KID BLACKBERRY KUSH

A bit nasty looking and fast acting. Born somewhere in Oregon in the early 1990s. Farmers seemed drawn to it due to its quick yields. Used mostly as medical pot on the West Coast. It's earthy with a slightly unpleasant sour taste. The scent will remind you of floral.

Sense: euphoric, sleepy, solitary

KILLER PURPLE

Around since the early days, Killer Purple is loved by old-school growers and smokers. The way it used to be. Enjoyed because of the strong, fast acting purple flowers.

At the beginning of the 1990s, Killer peeked its head into the British Columbia area, working its way south into Washington. Favored by farmers and home growers due to its ability to weather the weather. Unlike others, Killer has an old forest odor touched with some lavender.

Sense: euphoric, lazy, relaxed, sleepy, solitary

NEW FREEZELAND ORANGE

Combo of Afghani and Skunk, loved by smokers and the cash croppers with its really fast harvests. Popped up in the 1990s along the Northwest in the Bellingham area, and heading north to the mountains of British Columbia. Growers enjoyed its large harvests, creating it as a staple to many and Northwesters. Lemon, orange, and oak dominate your tongue. In the air, you'll smell orange and skunk.

Sense: happy, hungry, relaxed, sociable

LEMON DROP

Tough to find any real info on this gem. Like others born on the West Coast, but no one has claimed fame to this one. A lip smacker of lemon, equaled by the let's-do-something buzz.

Hard to find and not really grown by cash farmers, its days may be numbered. Sour tones in the mouth, mostly of lemon with the same lemony order.

Sense: attentive, energetic, euphoric, motivated

PLATINUM GIRL SCOUT COOKIES

Low yield for the growers, but huge, potent stuff from 2012, its sparkly appearance has been around. Gaining popularity everywhere, but costing a pretty penny. Getting her name by tasting like wonderful cookie dough, laced with grape, cinnamon, and even some pumpkin. Rounding off the experience with a grape like cookie dough odor filling the air.

Sense: euphoric, lazy, sleepy

HAZE HEAVEN

Most growers like its fast growing cycle, coming from a history of Afghan hash and Hawaii top plants. With an earthy tone, almost dirty and musky, With a harsh scent and sweeter taste.

Sense: happy, inspired, motivated

DOUBLE DIESEL

A double-hitting combination of NYC Diesel and Sour Diesel to create a one, two, flavor. If you like the diesel strain, Double lives up to its name. Very easy to grow, but not huge yields. Not sweet, with a musky taste with some earthy flavors. Like some diesels, it doesn't actually smell like diesel, more so sweet and fruity.

Sense: euphoric, happy, motivated, relaxed

SHIVA SKUNK

A tasty combo of Northern Lights and Skunk with an Amsterdam background. Shiva born in California, now everywhere. If you like Chinese food, you'll like the taste of this stuff, if you can get past the skunk smell.

Sense: aroused, creative, energetic, euphoric

PHANTON COOKIES

Just starting out in the halls of California, and getting more popular every day. Tasting like a minty, chocolate cookie with a bunch of earthy mixed in.

Sense: hungry, lazy, relaxed, sleepy

PRESIDENTIAL OG

From the sunny Southern California city of Los Angeles comes this very potent strain. Used mostly in medical dispensaries due to its potency. The odor of pine, lemon, finishing with an earthy skunk taste. Looking at the smoke you'll smell a citrus and flowers scent.

Sense: giggly, happy, hungry, relaxed, sleepy

MANGO HAZE

Having a nice smooth high, with a high use of curing aliments. Simply, this haze does not taste good. But with a fresh mango and peppermint, you'll enjoy the tropical feeling it gives you.

Sense: attentive, euphoric, relaxed, inspired

BOB MARLEY

Who knows where this one came from? It's a mystery, no clue. We do know this was Bob Marley's favorite smoke of choice. Very tasty with a fruity tropical taste and a scent of the same.

Sense: alert, creative, inspired

WILLIE NELSON

Spacey is a top note on this one. Taxes, Willie. Taxes.

Sense: euphoric, giggly, happy

What's in a Name?

With hundreds of strains available around the world, listing each one would entail a fairly large directory of its own. Below is a continued list of strains that might spark your interest. If nothing else, the names are great. Enjoy!

- Chiesel
- Elephant Stomper
- Emerald Jack
- Phishhead Kush
- Red Stem Afghani
- Albert Walker
- Girl Scout Cookies
- Kosher Kush
- Private Reserve
- Ewok
- Tahoe Alien
- Diesel
- 707 Headband
- G-13
- Jack Flash
- Heavy Duty Fruity
- Querkle
- MK Ultra
- OG Bubba Kush
- Grand Daddy Purple
- Jack Frost
- Casey Jones
- Black Domina
- White Queen
- Power Plant
- Orange Kush
- Durban Poison
- Afwreck
- Chemdawg
- Blue Dargon
- Sweet Tooth
- Golden Goat
- Sour Bubble
- God's Gift
- Purple Haze
- Space Queen
- Pineapple Express
- Banana Kush
- Lemon Kush
- Bubba Kush
- Grape Ape
- Blueberry Kush
- Hindu Kush
- Pineapple
- Super Skunk
- Afgooey
- Purple Urkle
- Blackberry Kush
- Jack Herer
- Cheese

- Skywalker
- Pure Kush
- Mr. Nice
- Blue Diesel
- Super Silver Haze
- Snow Cap Strain
- Wonder Woman
- White Widow
- White Russian
- White Rhino
- The Purps
- Silver Haze
- Romulan
- Pot of Gold
- Northern Lights
- Nebula
- Master Kush
- White Siberian
- Strawberry Ice
- Skunkberry
- Abusive OG
- Grape God
- Sour Mango
- Sweet Berry
- Silver Surfer
- Afghan Skunk
- Willy's Wonder
- Tahoe OG Kush
- Fucking Incredible
- Permafrost

- Space Bomb
- Black Jack
- Chernobyl
- Shiva
- Tangerine Dream
- White Lighting
- Bio Diesel
- Mean Green
- Sugar Kush
- THC Bomb
- Violator Kush
- Bubba
- Apollo 13
- Medicine Man
- Mango
- Lavender
- Kali Mist
- Ice
- Hash Plant
- Grape Kush
- Flo
- Chocolope
- Burmese Kush
- Bubble Gum
- Blue Moonshine
- Blue Cheese
- Blueberry
- Plum
- Green Queen
- Purple Voodoo

- God Bud
- Amnesia Haze
- Blockhead
- Purple Nepal
- Lavender Kush
- Sour Cheese
- XJ-13
- Agent Orange
- Vanilla Kush
- Bubbleberry
- Jilly Bean
- Super Jack
- Big Bud
- AK-48
- Platinum Kush
- Sage
- Black Widow
- AK-47
- Purple Kush
- OG Kush
- Sour Diesel
- Strawberry Cough
- LSD
- Afghan Kush
- Train Wreck
- Cherry Kush
- Cherry Pie
- Strawberry Kush
- Cannalope Haze
- UK Cheese

- Grapefruit
- Dutch Treat
- White Berry
- Cinderella 99
- Dream Queen
- Skunk
- Great White shark
- Cotton Candy
- Blueberry Skunk
- Maui Wowie
- Black Diamond
- Trinity
- Sour Kush
- Strawberry Diesel
- XXX OG
- Kandy Kush
- Berry White
- Orge Kush
- Red Diesel
- Sour Grape
- Red Dragon
- Hindu Skunk
- Orange Crush
- Blue Hawaiian
- Sour OG
- Fire OG
- True OG
- Blue Window
- Tahoe OG
- Platinum OG

- Tangerine
- Island Sweet Skunk
- NYC Diesel
- Green Crack
- Headband
- Blue Dream
- Alien OG
- Cough
- Blackberry
- Vortex
- Royal Kush
- Jack The Ripper
- Juicy Fruit
- Super Lemon Haze
- Acapulco Gold
- Death Star
- Super Sour Diesel
- Sensi Star
- LA Confidential
- Chocolate Chunk

Did I miss any?

If you'd like to have a name submitted on our website, go to the Weedgalized site (www.Weedgalized.com) and drop it off, we'll list it and give you credit.

Endnotes

Notes to Chapter 1

1. City of Fort Collins, Colorado Official Website, Amendment 64, Use and Regulation of Marijuana, "Ballot Title," http://www.fcgov.com/mmj/pdf/amendment64.pdf (accessed September 2, 2015).

2. Randy Wyrick, staff writer, "Could recreational marijuana business surpass ski industry," *Vail Daily*, April 29, 2014, http://www.vaildaily.com/news/regional/10616623-113/colorado-marijuana-cannabis-mitchem (accessed September 8, 2015).

Notes to Chapter 2

3. http://www.aboutmarijuana.com/marijuana_History.htm, (accessed September 8, 2015).

4. Colorado Department of Revenue: Permanent Rules Related to the Colorado Retail Marijuana Code, section C, 36, 48, https://www.colorado.gov/pacific/sites/default/files/Retail%20Marijuana%20Rules%2C%20Adopted%20090913%2C%20Effective%20101513%5B1%5D_0.pdf (accessed September 18, 2015).

5. Colorado Department of Revenue: Permanent Rules Related to the Colorado Retail Marijuana Code, section A, 42, 48, https://www.colorado.gov/pacific/sites/default/files/Retail%20Marijuana%20Rules%2C%20Adopted%20090913%2C%20Effective%20101513%5B1%5D_0.pdf (accessed September 18, 2015).

6. Colorado Department of Revenue: Permanent Rules Related to the Colorado Retail Marijuana Code, section D, 48, https://www.colorado.gov/pacific/sites/default/files/Retail%20Marijuana%20Rules%2C%20Adopted%20090913%2C%20Effective%20101513%5B1%5D_0.pdf (accessed September 18, 2015).

7. https://www.colorado.gov/pacific/marijuanainfo denver/residents-visitors, (accessed 11/24/15).

Notes to Chapter 4

8. Jean Harris, "Girl Scout sells cookies outside pot dispensary: 117 boxes in 2 hours," *Los Angeles Times*, February 21, 2014, www.latimes.com/food/dailydish/la-dd-girl-scout-sells-cookies-pot-clinic-20140221,0,174680.story#ixzz2zklYL6we (accessed September 8, 2015).

9. *Skunk Magazine*, http://www.skunkmagazine.com (accessed September 8, 2015).

10. *Cannabis Now Magazine*, http://cannabisnow magazine.com (accessed September 8,2015).

11. *Ladybud Magazine*, http://www.ladybud.com (accessed September 8,2015).

12. *Releaf Magazine*, http://releaf.co/?page_id=1100 (accessed September 8,2015).

13. Cultivating Spirits Tour Company, http://cultivatingspirits.com (accessed September 8,2015).

Notes to Chapter 5

14. www.munchandco.com/#about (accessed November 9, 2015).

15. Bill Chappell, "Marijuana Vending Machine Unveiled in Colorado," NPR, April 13, 2014, http://www.npr.org/sections/thetwo-way/2014/04/13/302551086/marijuana-vending-machine-unveiled-in-colorado (accessed September 8, 2015).

Notes to Chapter 6

16. Robert Hunter et al., *The Grateful Dead: The Illustrated Trip*, (London, England: DK, 2003).

Notes to Chapter 7

17. For current information on obtaining a budtender "Support Badge" go to https://www.colorado.gov/pacific/enforcement/Medical%20Marijuana%20Occupational%20Licensing (accessed September 8, 2015).

Notes to Chapter 8

18. Timothy Ferriss, *The 4-Hour Chef: The Simple Path to Cooking Like a Pro, Learning Anything, and Living the Good Life*, (US: New Harvest, 2012).

19. Jack Herer, *The Emperor Wears No Clothes: Hemp and the Marijuana Conspiracy . . . and How Hemp Can Save the World!*,(Austin, TX: AH HA Publishing, 2010).

20. United States District Court for the District of Colorado, http://www.safestreetsalliance.org.php54-2.dfw1-2.websitetestlink.com/assets/media/New_Vision_Complaint.pdf (accessed September 8, 2015).

21. Native Roots Mission Statement, https://nativeroots303.com/about/mission-statement (accessed September 8, 2015).

Notes to Chapter 10

22. "About the Cannabist," http://www.thecannabist.co/about/ (accessed September 8, 2015).

23. Mitch Dickman, Director, Katie Shapiro, Producer, *Rolling Papers: A Documentary Film* by Mitch Dickman, March 2015, http://www.rollingpapersfilm.com/filmmakers (accessed September 8, 2015)

24. Seth Rogen, "Rogen invites moviegoers to get 'baked' with him at screening," *Toronto Sun*, November 27, 2014, http://www.torontosun.com/2014/11/27/seth-rogen-invites-moviegoers-to-get-baked-with-him-at-screening (accessed September 8, 2015).

Notes to Chapter 11

25. Maureen Dowd, "Don't Harsh Our Mellow, Dude," *New York Times*, June 4, 2014, http://www.nytimes.com/2014/06/ 04/opinion/dowd-dont-harsh-our-mellow-dude.html?_r=1 (accessed September 9, 2015).

Notes to Chapter 12

26. Jack Herer Quote, http://www.brainyquote.com/quotes/quotes/j/jackherer358435.html (accessed October 2, 2015).

27. Regulate Marijuana, "Impact on the Consumer," http://www.regulatemarijuana.org/marijuana-vs-alcohol (accessed September 9, 2015).

28. Leah Miranda, "Alcohol Vs Marijuana," *Recovery First*, March 4, 2013, http://www.recoveryfirst.org/alcohol-vs-marijuana (accessed September 9, 2015).

Notes to Chapter 13

29. Katie Kuntz, "Colorado's Marijuana Enforcement Division releases new rules for medical, retail marijuana businesses," *Grand Junction Free Press* in partnership with Rocky Mountain PBS I-News, September 29, 2014, http://www.gjfreepress.com/news/grandjunction/13219883-113/marijuana-rules-testing-medical (accessed September 9, 2015).

30. L.V. Anderson, "The United Sweets of America," *Slate Magazine*, August 24, 2014, http://www.slate.com/articles/life/food/2014/08/united_sweets_of_america_map_a_dessert_for_every_state_in_the_country.html (accessed September 9, 2015).

31. Kristin Wyatt (The Associated Press), "State putting up $8M to study marijuana's medical potential," *Summit Daily*, December 18, 2014, http://www.summitdaily.com/news/14281296-113/marijuana-colorado-medical-research (accessed September 9, 2015).

32. "Native Americans Granted Legalization of Marijuana on Reservation Lands," *High Times*, December 11, 2014, http://www.hightimes.com/read/native-americans-granted-legalization-marijuana-reservation-lands (accessed September 9, 2015).

Notes to Chapter 14

33. Alexandra Klausner, "Pot-friendly Denver saw a 73 percent increase in hotel searches since last year as Easter weekend falls on April 20, the nation's unofficial marijuana holiday," *Daily Mail*, April 18, 2014, http://www.dailymail.co.uk/news/article-

2608157/Pot-friendly-Denver-saw-73-percent-
increase-hotel-searches-year-Easter-weekend-falls-
April-20-nations-unofficial-marijuana-holiday.html
#ixzz3kFAPq5yT (accessed September 9, 2015).

Notes to Chapter 15

34. Neal Pollack, "Neal Pollack's Reefer Roadtrip from
    Texas to Free America (aka Colorado)," *The
    Cannabist,* January 5, 2015, http://www.thecannabist.
    co/2015/01/05/neal-pollacks-weed-loving-roadtrip-
    texas-free-america-aka-colo, (accessedSeptember 7,
    2015).

35. Pandora® Radio, http://www.pandora.com (accessed
    September 9, 2015).

36. Rocky Mountain High Intensity Drug Trafficking
    Area, http://www.rmhidta.org (accessed September
    9, 2015).

37. "Epilepsy Patients Flock To Colorado After Medical
    Pot Gives Them Hope," CBS4, November 18, 2013,
    http://denver.cbslocal.com/2013/11/18/epilepsy-
    patients-flocking-to-colorado-after-medical-pot-
    gives-them-hope (accessed September 9, 2015).

38. Epilepsy Foundation COLORADO, "CARERS Act
    Introduced in the Senate," July 2015, www.epilepsy-
    colorado.org/index.php?s=12107 (accessed
    September 9, 2015).

Appendix II

39. Bruce Brown, District Attorney, Fifth Judicial
    District, Clear Creek, Eagle, Lake, and Summit
    Counties, in conjunction with Summit County

Law Enforcement, Chief Mark Heminghous, Dillon Police Department, Chief Mark Hanschmidt, Silverthorne Police Department, Chief Shannon Haynes, Breckenridge Police Department, Sheriff John Minor, Summit County Sheriff's office, and Chief Tom Wickman, Frisco Police Department.

Glossary of Terms

40. *Trends in Pharmacological Sciences,* Volume 30, Issue 10, October 2009, 515–527, http://www. sciencedirect.com/ science/journal/01656147/ 30/10 (accessed September 9, 2015).

Glossary of Terms

Glossary created with the help of the staff of
Native Roots dispensary in Frisco, CO.

420, 4:20, or 4/20: Originating in California as the time people would meet by a statue to smoke pot. The term or phrase means "to smoke pot" or to reference the use of marijuana. Example: 420-friendly housing means the landlord or hotel is okay with the use of marijuana on the premises.

420 Friendly: Cannabis friendly.

BHO: A concentrated cannabis wax extract made by pushing liquid butane through a tube packed with either trim or full nuggets of cannabis.

Baked: Getting really high or stoned.

Blazed: Being or getting super high.

Blunt: Hollowed-out cigar or any tobacco leaf filled with marijuana.

Bong: A water pipe.

Budtender: A person who stands behind the counter at a dispensary and sells marijuana and cannabis-infused products. They are knowledgeable and well versed in all things cannabis. They act as guides to the world of cannabis by teaching proper consumption and answering questions.

Cannasseur: This term is a combination of the two words cannabis and connoisseur. One who consumes and enjoys cannabis, and studies the many different nuances, flavors, smells, and terpenes.

Caregiver (Medical Marijuana caregiver): Caregivers are entitled to manufacture or possess medical marijuana in order to provide that medicine to a person holding a medical marijuana card.

CBC (Cannabichromene): Cannabinoid from cannabis.*

CBD (Cannabidiol): Cannabinoid from cannabis. *

CBG (Cannabigerol): Cannabinoid from cannabis. *

CBN (Cannabinol): Cannabinoid from cannabis.*

* For more information on the above four terms refer
  to Trends in Pharmacological Sciences.[40]

Cannabinoids: Chemical compounds unique to cannabis that produce various effects, such as pain management/relief. The most abundant and well known is THC (tetrahydro-cannabinol). There are over eighty-five cannabinoids.

Cannabis Cup: The world's preeminent Cannabis festival, which was founded in 1987 by Steven Hager, also called the High Times Cannabis Cup. Judges at the festival vote for the best strain of cannabis, best new product, best booth, best glass, and best hash.

Clone/cloning: Cutting and rooting a healthy shoot of a marijuana plant, which helps to keep gender-specific growing.

Contact high: The act of getting high without actually consuming cannabis by inadvertently inhaling secondhand pot smoke. This is more prone to happen in enclosed areas. *See hot box.*

Couch locked: An intense high that keeps you in the couch longer than normal. Users have reported not being able to get up off the couch for hours.

Dab/dabbing: A dab is a slang term used to refer to a dose of concentrates. Dabbing is the act of administering concentrated form of cannabis via vape pen, rig, or other apparatus.

Edibles: Foods that have been infused with cannabis extracts, most likely baked goods such as brownies and cookies. They can also be in candies, gummy squares, breads, and beverages. Can be made from clippings, stems, leaves, and trim from leftovers.

Flower: The dense part of the budding marijuana plant that contains the highest concentration of active cannabinoids.

Grows or a grow: A facility for indoor growing of marijuana.

Gummies: Usually squares or rounds of chewy candy infused with cannabis.

Hash: Short for hashish. The resin from the buds/flowers of the cannabis plant.

Hash explosions: Dangerous explosions from using butane to heat and extract concentrates.

Hot box: Sitting inside a car or other small, enclosed space, and smoking marijuana, thus filling the space with smoke so every breath is a hit. Also called clambake or receiving a contact high.

Hybrid: A strain of cannabis containing both *indica* and *sativa* qualities.

Indica: One of the three different varieties of cannabis. Usually the plants are shorter and the effect is that of a full-bodied feeling of relaxation. Also used as a pain reliever.

Kief: Crystals and little crumbs of weed that fall off from grinding marijuana and accumulate over time.

Kush: A strain of cannabis that originated from the Hindu-Kush Mountains. Original Kush was full *indica*.

Live resin: Whole fresh/wet plant extraction that captures a higher terpene level.

Nugg: Slang for a nugget, bud, or flower of cannabis.

Reclaim: Residue left in rig after dabbing.

Rig: Dabbing rig or dabbing bong. An apparatus used for dabbing.

Sativa: One of three varieties of cannabis with taller plants and longer, slender leaves, the effect of which is more uplifting and euphoric.

Shatter: Type of concentrate made with trim or whole nuggets of cannabis and extracted and purged in a vacuum oven. It is typically hardened and has an amber-like color.

Solar hit: Using a magnifying glass and the sun to light the weed while smoking it.

Strain: When referring to marijuana, it means type of marijuana or cannabis.

Terpenes: Simple organic molecules that are present in living organisms. When referring to cannabis, these are what enable marijuana enthusiasts to smell different fragrances and flavor profiles.

THC (Tetrahydrocannabinol): The psychoactive ingredient in marijuana.

Tinctures: A solution of alcohol or alcohol and water, containing animal, vegetable, or chemical drugs, including that of cannabis.

Vape pen: A smoking apparatus that allows consumption of cannabis by vaporizing in a heating chamber.

Weedgalized: When a state takes the final step and legalizes recreational marijuana and an onslaught of fascinating stories ensue that need to be told in an awesome book. A portmanteau by Johnny Welsh.

Wax: (Also called wax concentrate) A potent form of marijuana that can contain up to 80 percent THC. A form of concentrate also known as flake. Wax gets its color and texture from a whipping type process.

Bibliography

Barcott, Bruce. *Weed the People: The Future of Legal Marijuana in America*. New York: Time Books, 2015.

Ferriss, Timothy. *The 4-Hour Chef: The Simple Path to Cooking Like a Pro, Learning Anything, and Living the Good Life*, US: New Harvest, 2012.

Herer, Jack. *The Emperor Wears No Clothes: Hemp and the Marijuana Conspiracy . . . and How Hemp Can Save the World!* Austin: AH HA Publishing, 2010.

Hunter, Robert et al. *The Grateful Dead: The Illustrated Trip*. London: DK, 2003.

Resources

Baca, Ricardo. *The Cannabist*. Denver: *The Denver Post*.
    http://www.thecannabist.co.

Cannabis Now Magazine.
    http://cannabisnowmagazine.com.

Colorado Department of Revenue: Marijuana Enforcement
    Division. "Permanent Rules Related to the Colorado
    Retail Marijuana Code." https://www.colorado.gov/
    pacific/sites/default/files/Retail%20Marijuana%20Rules
    %2C%20Adopted%20090913%2C%20Effective%
    20101513%5B1%5D_0.pdf
    (accessed September 18, 2015).

Cultivating Spirits Tour Company.
    http://cultivatingspirits.com.

High Times. http://www.hightimes.com.

Ladybud Magazine. http://www.ladybud.com.

MARIJUANA. http://www.marijuana.com/strains.

Native Roots Colorado. Marijuana Dispensary.
    https://nativeroots303.com.

NORML. http://norml.org/aboutmarijuana.

Releaf Magazine. http://releaf.co/?page_id=1100.

Skunk Magazine. http://www.skunkmagazine.com.

About the Author

John J. Welsh (a.k.a. Johnny Welsh)

Johnny Welsh has worked as a professional bartender in Frisco, Colorado, for almost twenty years. Born in Atlantic City, New Jersey, he graduated from Syracuse University with a degree in Italian Language, Literature, and Culture.

After working in a graduate study program in Italy, he moved back to the east coast to pursue his dream of writing music and playing in a band. When that scene got a little too crazy, he retreated to the heart of beautiful Colorado ski country.

Since Colorado legalized marijuana in 2014, no one has heard more tales from such a wide assortment of shifty, funny, entrepreneurial, and "enlightened" characters than Johnny the bartender.

Contribute Your Stories: Submit Now for Volume 2

Weedgalized: Part Deux

Don't forget, we always welcome new stories, funny incidents, and unique new businesses that have happened as a result of the legalization of recreational marijuana. We need stories for the new section called Colorado stoner confessions. If you have one to tell or share, visit www.Weedgalized.com and submit your story. It just might be chosen for the next volume in this series.

"Pass it on!"

Quick Order Form

Email orders: Weedgalized@yahoo.com

Website orders: www.Weedgalized.com

Telephone orders and bulk discounts: 1-970-389-0238

**Weedgalized in Colorado: True Tales From the
    High Country** **$19.95**

Shipping by air: US: $4.00 for first book and $1.00 for each additional book. Bulk discounts for five or more.

Use the form on the following page and mail to:
Peak 1 Publishing, LLC
Po Box 2046
Frisco, CO 80443
USA
Telephone: 1-970-389-0238

Weedgalized in Colorado:
True Tales From the High Country

Quantity_____ X $19.95=_____ plus shipping=_____

Name_____

Address_____

City _____ State_____ Zip Code_____

Telephone__(____)_____

Email_____

Visa_____ MasterCard_____ Discover_____

Card Number_____

Name on card_____

Exp. Date_____

Or send check made payable to Peak 1 Publishing, LLC

Weedgalized in Colorado:
True Tales From the High Country

Quantity_____ X $19.95=_____ plus shipping=_____

Name_____

Address_____

City _____ State _____ Zip Code_____

Telephone__ (_____) _____

Email_____

Visa_____   MasterCard_____   Discover_____

Card Number_____

Name on card_____

Exp. Date_____

Or send check made payable to Peak 1 Publishing, LLC

Follow the blog on
www.Weedgalized.com